The Power of Sand

Burnett County and the Civilian Conservation Corps

by Carole M. Fure

Burnett County Historical Society

TRAVEL BACK THRU TIME

with the Burnett County Historical Society which provides educational experiences that foster an understanding of historical relationships, encourage the critical examination of values, ideas, and actions and support open free inquiry and dialogue.

©2004 Burnett County Historical Society

All rights reserved. No part of this publication may be reproduced or transmitted in any form or by any means, electronic or mechanical, including photocopying, recording or any information storage and retrieval system, without permission in writing from the publisher.

First Edition: May 2004

5 4 3 2 1

BURNETT COUNTY HISTORICAL SOCIETY
8500 County Road U
Danbury, Wisconsin 54830
USA
715-866-8890 • www.theforts.org • fahp@centurytel.net

Includes Riverside CCC Camp Roster.
ISBN 0-9753447-0-6

Printed in Duluth, Minnesota

Design: Mathew Pawlak
Editor: Carole M. Fure
Printing: ProPrint, Duluth, Minnesota, United States of America

Cover: Ivol Paulus, a 1939 Riverside CCC Camp enrollee, inspects tree plantings.

Acknowledgements

This book began quite simply with a research request. Charles Tollander and Michael Myers wanted to know more about the Riverside CCC Camp in Burnett County in preparation for a dedication of the camp site. I agreed to do the research. As I delved into the records, the story captured me. I could not let it go until it was told. Thus this book was created.

There are many unknown individuals who, by preserving historical records, assisted in the writing of this book. Among these are the Burnett County Historical Society, Grantsburg Historical Society, Inter-County Leader Archives, River Falls Area Research Center, Wisconsin State Historical Society, National Archives and Records Administration in Chicago, and the Civilian Personnel Records Center in St. Louis.

Research requires finding and reviewing thousands of documents. Wayne and Nancy Burmeister and May Schultz searched through boxes of papers looking for relevant material. With their assistance a difficult task became much easier.

Paul Sexton located CCC men for me to interview. My special thanks to Byron Baker, Myron Dahl, John Dunn, Norris Hoag, Bert Lund, Warren Melin, Roy Nordquist, Ivol Paulus, Charles Scotka, Duane Sandberg, Harvard Stengal, and Russell Stewart for sharing their stories.

Dotty Gooding, Maurice Heyer, Nancy Jappe, Donna Jones, Linda Potter, May Schultz, and Phil Stromberg reviewed the manuscript. Their invaluable insights and suggestions provided accuracy and clarity to the book.

My deepest appreciation goes to Mrs. Helen Quigley for donating John Quigley's CCC photo collection to the Burnett County Historical Society. These pictures speak a thousand words and give the story life.

Mathew Pawlak prepared the manuscript for printing. His professional graphic design skills massaged a rough manuscript into a beautiful book.

My family, John, Dave, and Deb, listened and supported me in this project. I'm sure at times they wished I could find something else to talk about.

As this project comes full circle I owe special thanks to Michael and Diane Myers and Charles and Eunice Tollander for financially supporting the printing of the book, thus bringing this project to a successful completion. Proceeds from the book will be used to support future publications.

Table of Contents

Acknowledgements		iii
Introduction		v
Section 1	Evolution	1
Section 2	Settlement and Abandonment	3
Section 3	Problems and Solutions	6
Section 4	The Depression	9
Section 5	Birth of the CCC	10
Section 6	Enrollment	12
Section 7	Rookies	14
Section 8	Conservation Projects	21
Section 9	Forest Protection	22
Section 10	Buildings and Parks Construction	29
Section 11	Forest Development	30
Section 12	Lake and Stream Improvement	33
Section 13	Wildlife Management	38
Section 14	Community Service	39
Section 15	Riverside Camp Life	41
Section 16	Education	49
Section 17	Sports - Recreation - Leisure	52
Section 18	Benefits	58
Section 19	John Quigley and the CCC	63
Section 20	The Final Years	65
Section 21	Civilian Conservation Corps Rosters	69
Works Consulted		83
Endnotes		85
About the Author		90

Introduction

The Civilian Conservation Corps (CCC) arrived in Burnett County in a time of crisis - a time when citizens were grappling with the unintended consequences of previous choices, a time when they had not yet recovered from laws which hog-tied prudent action, a time when tax delinquency was the only escape. Difficult times in the county became more difficult when the Great Depression struck.

No event stands alone but is molded by the past and influences the future. The pre-depression struggles of the county foreshadowed the coming of the Civilian Conservation Corps. The Great Depression was the catalyst that brought the CCC to Burnett County. The Riverside CCC story carries us from the burdened past to a hope-filled future.

The future of Burnett County and the CCC boys was found in caring for the land rather than in conquering it. Their guardianship bound the boys to the land in an extraordinary partnership. They nurtured the land, and the land nourished them. They knew what it meant to be alive - really alive. The CCC boys grew strong in spirit and were forever changed by their experience.

The CCC story demonstrates the influence of attitude in determining the quality of life. Hindsight, a gift from the ages, gives us the opportunity to learn from the past. With age comes wisdom, but sometimes age comes alone.

Evolution

Section 1

The story of the Civilian Conservation Corps begins 10,000 to 20,000 years ago when the Superior lobe of the Wisconsin glacier pulverized Canadian rocks into sand and deposited them, up to 80 feet deep,[1] across most of Burnett County. As the climate warmed, the glacier melted in retreat leaving behind 10 rivers, 508 lakes[2] and many wooded swamps and open marshes.

The seasons as we know them today developed over the next 10,000 years as the climate continued to warm. Located in the interior of a large continent, without the temperature-moderating effects of the oceans, the county is subjected to significant weather changes. Westerly currents pull cold dry air masses from the Arctic across the county in winter and warm moist air masses from the Gulf in summer.

Cloudy, cold, and snowy winters begin in November and last through March.[3] January is the coldest month with a mean temperature of 10 degrees, and July is the warmest month with an average temperature of 68 degrees. The annual mean precipitation is 30 inches.[4] The record low temperature for Wisconsin, a minus 54 degrees, was recorded at Danbury in 1922.[5]

EXTENT OF ORIGINAL BRUSH-PRAIRIE

DOUGLAS
BAYFIELD
ORIGINAL BRUSH-PRAIRIE
BURNETT
WASHBURN
POLK

Nutrient poor and drought prone soil, combined with fire, shaped the landscape of the county. Predictable fire intervals of 15 to 20 years, encouraged by dead dry grasses and the flammability of pine, discouraged the survival of upright, woody trees and shrubs. Isolated pines, escaping the frequent light burning over a sufficient time, were able to grow to maturity creating a pine savanna/brush prairie. A pine savanna/brush prairie is described as consisting mostly of jack and red pine (approximately eight per acre), brush (mostly oak), and prairie grasses. White pine forests grew along the southern edge of the county where soils were more fertile, in areas where clay sub-soils helped to retain moisture, and along river edges where fires were abated.[6]

For 2,000 years this was the home of Woodland Indians. Dependent upon the environment, they traveled with the seasons to hunt, trap, fish, and gather. They learned from their

The pine savanna/brush prairie (barrens) covered all of the county except the towns of Roosevelt, Trade Lake, and Wood River, the southern halves of Daniels, Dewey, LaFollette, and Siren, and the section of Blaine west of the St. Croix River.[7]

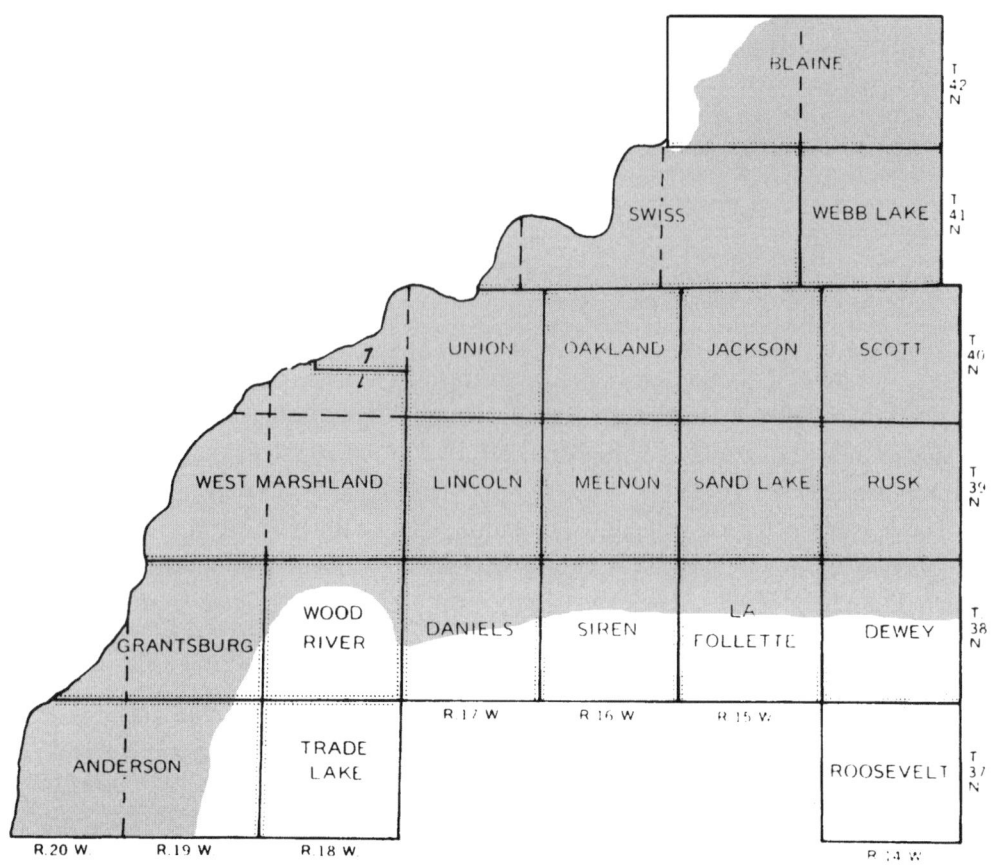

ancestors, passed down from generation to generation, the use of each plant and animal, where to find them, when and how to harvest. They were careful not to consume or damage the source of their sustenance. Their very existence depended on it.

This place not only nurtured bodies but also spirits. George Nelson, clerk for the XY Fur Company on the Yellow River in 1802, described his feelings.

> *Whenever this country becomes settled how delightfully will the inhabitants pass their time. There is no place perhaps on this globe where nature has displayed & diversified land & water as here. I always felt as if invited to settle down & admire the beautiful views with a sort of joyful thankfulness for having been led to them...Nature is here calm, placid & serene, as if telling man, in language mute, indeed, — not addressed to the Ears, but to heart & Soul: It is here man is happy.[8]*
> *A Winter in the St. Croix Valley*

Section 2

Settlement and Abandonment

The first settlers saw the beauty of this land. They also saw the possibility of prosperity. Logging operators striped the land of its timber and then sold the land or abandoned it to the delinquent tax rolls. Cleared land and the open nature of the barrens attracted early farmers.

In 1902 the Burnett County Board of Immigration issued a book promoting Burnett County as an agricultural paradise. A lengthy article, titled "The Unlimited Agricultural Resources of the Entire Northern Part of the State," extolled the advantages of settling in the county.

Deserted homesteads dotted the country side as the short growing and stingy soil forced settlers to abandon their dreams.

That these meadows were at one time lakes is quite certain. There are a number of little lakes scattered about through these meadows but they are all shallow and when the meadows are properly ditched these lakes will undoubtedly dry up...turning them into good farms.[9]

Before farmers could plow under the native grasses to plant alfalfa, alfalfa engineered in Madison to grow in stingy soil and cool climates, they first had to clear the land of stumps, slash and brush. The 1921 Burnett County Board of Supervisors considered land clearing an important project for the year. They distributed 15,000 pounds of TNT, equivalent to 20,250 pounds of dynamite, to farmers throughout the county. The farmers were charged only 30 percent of the cost of the explosives. In addition to explosives, all types of apparatus, to assist in advancing the cause, were designed and demonstrated.

Many People See Stumps Go
More than one thousand people turned out on the 17th of August to see the land clearing demonstration staged at Siren... The interest which is being shown in these demonstrations indicates that people are being aroused to the fact that more land cleared is patriotism.
Burnett County Enterprise August 23, 1917

The University of Wisconsin's College of Agriculture threw its influence behind the settlement movement. They conducted agricultural experiments and held institutes to assist farmers in their attempts to cultivate sandy soils in a cold climate. Burnett County's normal growing season was 120 days, 40 days shorter than in the southern part of the state. They conducted experiments to develop early-maturing soybeans, peas, and corn. They attempted to modify new crops such as kudzu and sunflowers for silage. They made special efforts to refine dairy techniques for northern uses.[10]

North Town of Blaine
A.S. Keating raised some very fine strawberries and is sharing them with the neighbors to encourage them to go and do likewise. We think a good deal of our claims and think it only requires labor to make productive homes. Journal of Burnett County July 15, 1904

Persuasive advertising, ingenious methods of land clearing, expert advice, and enormous individual effort were not enough to overcome the natural elements of harsh weather, short growing season, and sterile soils. From the turn of the century into the 1940's, farmers struggled to survive. Chuck Scotka, a long-retired farmer from Oakland Township, responded to a question about the difficulty of farming sandy soil. "No." He replied. "We did OK. We sold rocks to Hopkins." In spite of everyone's efforts, mortgages flourished, crops failed and farmers abandoned their dreams to the delinquent tax rolls.

TO HOMESEEKERS.

The good lands of Burnett county that are cheap are in the northern part. I am located at Lilly Lake, in town 41, range 14, and my postoffice address is Spooner, Wis. If you want a homestead, railroad land, timber lands, or any kind of lands come and see me. I can fix you out with what you want, if it is to be found. Write or come and see me.   A. L. McDowell.

Farms For Sale.

Now is the time to buy a farm. Before you buy let me show you what I have to offer. I have farms in all parts of the county, at all kinds of prices and easy terms. I have good hardwood timber lands for sale cheap, also a complete stock of lumber, lath and shingles   J. H. Jensen.
Grantsburg, Wis.

Section 2 - Settlement and Abandonment

Tax delinquent farms were sold and resold creating a merry-go-round of settlement, delinquency, resettlement, new delinquency.

Swiss
A general exodus from this country seems to be threatening and many have already gone. Correspondent advises growing rye on meadows not quite in shape. Unidentified Newspaper Clipping from 1910

Delinquent taxes placed a burden on the county. Under Wisconsin tax procedure, all those who received revenue from the county taxes received their share first. The county received its share of the revenue last and therefore had to absorb the shortage in uncollected taxes. The county made up the shortfall through the sale of delinquent tax land.[11] This practice created a merry-go-round of settlement, then delinquency, resettlement, new delinquency and so on. The land entering the delinquent tax rolls increased as the land sold from the rolls decreased. By 1927 the wave of tax delinquency became formidable and threatened to submerge the county.

5

Section 3

Problems and Solutions

- Burnett County total area 572,726 acres.
- Surface water area 41,600 acres.
- County Forest 106,330 acres.
- State Land 69,184 acres.
- U.S. Government Land 6,948 acres.
- Farm Land 82,742 acres.

2003 BURNETT COUNTY ALMANAC

Inappropriate use of the land for agriculture and ill-conceived taxation laws were the root of the problem. The land was best suited for growing trees, and trees were needed as the inexhaustible forests were nearly depleted. Because pines require fewer nutrients, they do well in acidic soils.[12] No one however, was interested in growing trees, because inappropriate laws taxed all lands equally, although revenue from a tree harvest would not be seen for many years.

In 1905, under the direction of Edward Griffith, Wisconsin's first state forester, the state began buying up delinquent lands for a forest reserve. In 1915, however, the State Supreme Court ruled the policy unconstitutional. It was not until 1924, nine years later that the state legislature amended the constitution, permitting the state to appropriate funds for forestry and waterpower. The following year the Wisconsin Legislature authorized the federal purchase of state lands.[13]

The state, however, could not own and manage all the lands available for forest development. Forestry had to involve private landowners. A constitutional amendment modifying the "uniform rule of taxation" led to the enactment of the Forest Crop Law in 1927. Under its terms, the owner was relieved of property taxes except for an annual charge of ten cents an acre. In return, he was obliged to pay a severance tax of 10 percent of the value of the timber when cut. In lieu of the property taxes that a town might have received, the state was to pay ten cents per acre per year for lands entered under the law.[14]

In 1929 the Forest Crop Law was extended to include counties. The Conservation Department contributed 10 cents per acre for the development of county forests. When the timber was harvested from the county forests, the state would claim 75 percent, a reimbursement of its earlier contribution.

Burnett County had collected a significant amount of delinquent tax land when the lands could not be sold. According to Will T. Malone, chairman of the Burnett County Board of Commissioners in 1932, the county began taking delinquent tax certificates in 1927. Burnett County had its first lands, 30,230 acres, accepted under Forest Crop Law in March 1932. February 6, 1933 the Burnett County Board of Commissioners established a county forest.[15]

The new forests needed protection from fire, the natural event that for centuries had kept the area a brush prairie. Although settlers were already engaged in fighting fires, concerned with the loss of life and business, they did not worry about young forests and wildlife. In 1927, the Conservation Commission assigned Fire Protection Districts with the responsibility for fire control. Burnett County was located in Fire Protection District #2 and was under the direction of Philip A. McDonald. McDonald constructed windmill-type fire towers and strung a single line ground circuit telephone system through the trees to connect the towers to firefighters.[16]

Section 3 - Problems and Solutions

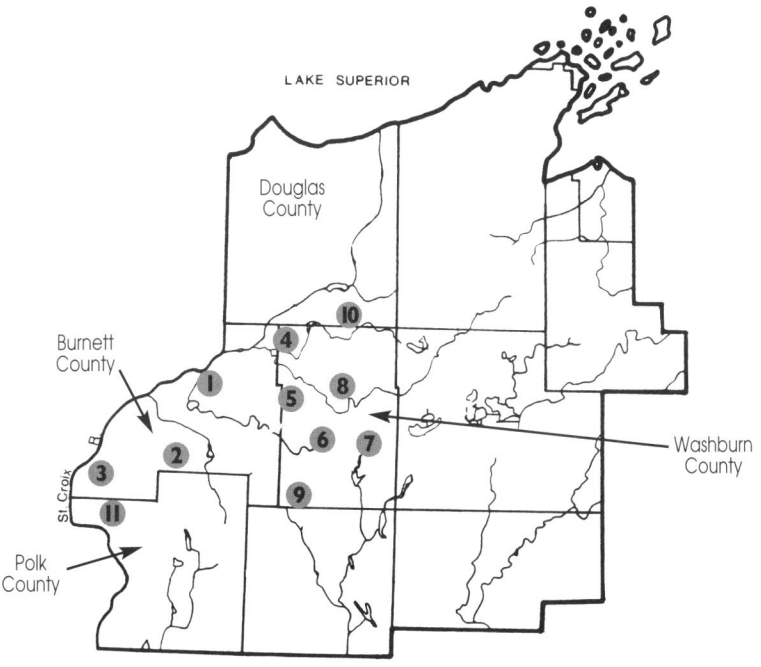

Fire Protection District #2. Lookout towers were located at Danbury 1, Siren 2 and Grantsburg 3 in Burnett County; Five Mile 4 and McKenzie 5 on the Burnett-Washburn County line; Issabella 6, Potato Lake 7, Lampson 8, and Barronett 9 in Washburn County, Gordon 10 in Douglas County and Sterling 11 in Polk County.[17]

Land clearing was the number one cause of fires[18] and actually increased their destructive nature. By increasing the fuel, they intensified the fire's heat.

With the adoption of the Forest Crop Law and fire protection services, the nation was assured a new beginning in forestry. As forestlands increased a new problem arose, the isolation of settlers. Providing services to secluded areas placed a financial burden on the county. The proposed solution was to relocate isolated settlers and to pass zoning laws to prevent re-settlement.

Reasons Why Land Zoning Would Be of Benefit To County Taxpayers
Cut-over land with scattered agricultural settlement and heavy tax delinquency have brought land use problems to Burnett County. Tax delinquency is primarily associated with non-productive land, concentrated on certain soils and areas. Wherever settlement is sparse the costs of schools, roads and other public services are high per capita, per pupil or per $1000 of valuation. A settler may cost the community, the county, and the state more in one year than he will pay in taxes in 20 years. Relocating settlers, but even if this is done what is to prevent others from going in. Journal of Burnett County May 31, 1934

In August 1929, the Wisconsin Legislature passed a bill that provided counties with the authority to zone rural land. Burnett County's Zoning Ordinance was enacted in 1935. It created three land-use districts, Forestry, Recreation and Unrestricted. Under this ordinance, nearly 111,000 acres of land, 20 percent of the land area of the county, was closed to future agricultural settlement and yearlong residence.[19]

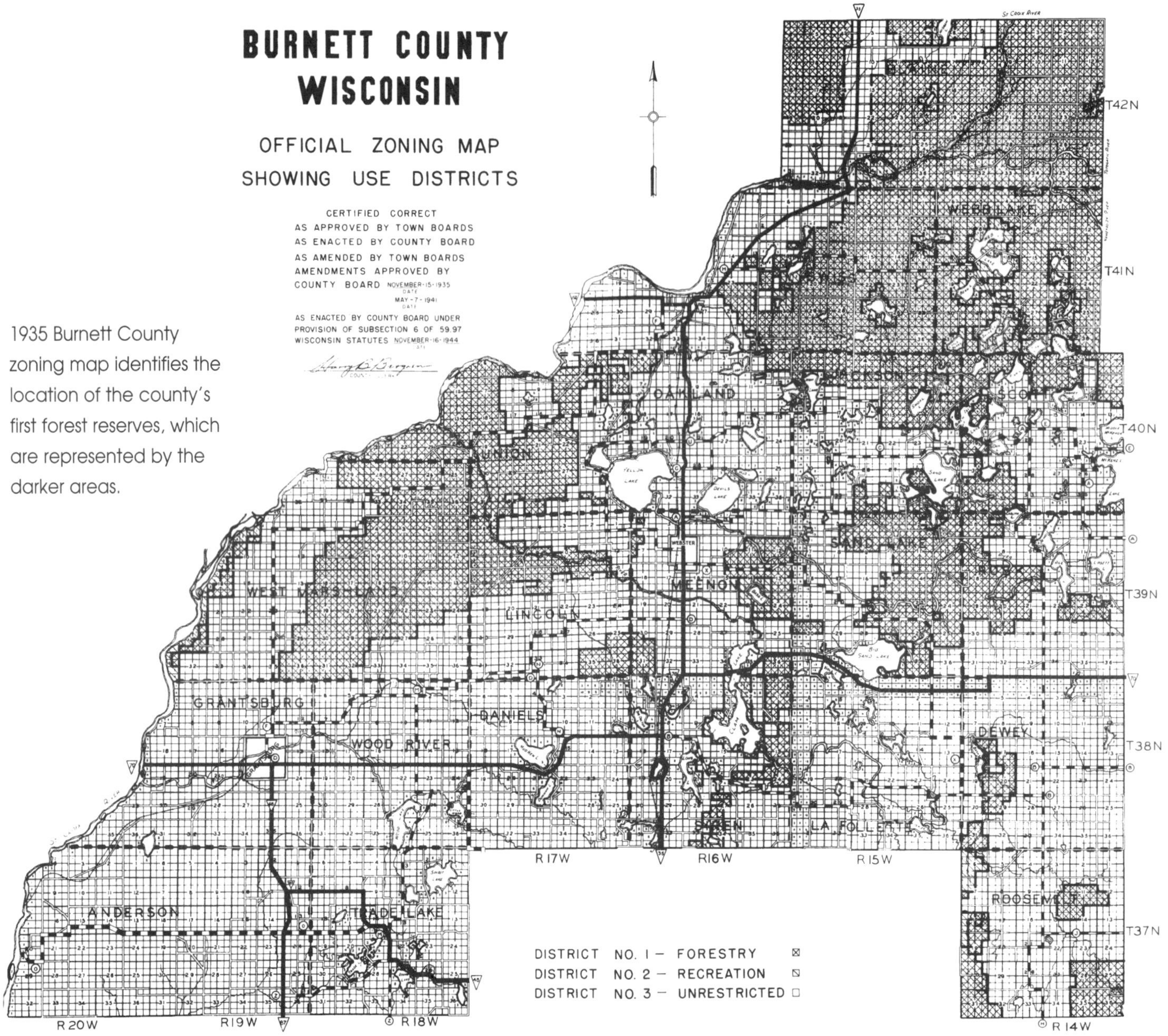

The Power of Sand – Burnett County Civilian Conservation Corps

1935 Burnett County zoning map identifies the location of the county's first forest reserves, which are represented by the darker areas.

A program to assist the isolated and impoverished farm families of the cutover area to reestablish themselves in more prosperous places was established through the Wisconsin Forest-Farm Homestead.[20]

Forest Home School District Is Dissolved
(Included the Aspen and Lee School Areas)
This action was taken because of the small number of students and residents in the district. The county has purchased the property for forest croplands and after July 1 there will be no one residing there.
Journal of Burnett County April 28, 1938

Section 4

The Depression

The citizens of the county now had the means to dig their way out from under the burdens of the past. Provisions were in place for the state and federal government to appropriate county land, for local government and private property owners to receive forest tax relief, for increased forest fire protection and for the enactment of zoning regulations. All of this, however, was in its infancy when, on October 29, 1929, the Great Depression struck. The downward spiral of the county accelerated.

Scorching temperatures, record cold snaps, drought, and wind erosion destroyed crops and hope. Marginal farmers were no longer marginal. Their lands joined other lands on the delinquent tax rolls. Tax delinquency rose from 68 percent in 1931 to 84 percent in 1932[21] tripling its pre-depression levels.

> **Burnett County Delinquency Is 93,000 Acres**
> *Eighty percent of wild and cutover lands are delinquent. The heavy land tax delinquency in Burnett County the past three years has reached an alarming proportion...There is but little demand or inquiry for these lands as the county has been able to dispose of only 1,500 acres the past two years.*
> Journal of Burnett County December 29, 1932

> **Over 50 Per Cent Registered Needy Placed At Work**
> *Ray Larrabee, manager of the Burnett county national reemployment office, reports exactly 2,416 persons have registered for employment from September 22, 1933 to February 1, 1934. This is 23.6 percent of Burnett County's population of 10,233.*
> Journal of Burnett County March 1, 1934

The county citizens established organizations for the relief of the poor. The objective was to care for the needy locally, keeping them off the federal and, if possible, the local dole. Neighbor helped neighbor. County Commissioners reduced their salaries, and some townships levied no local taxes. Schools, receiving only 54 percent of the state aid due them, decreased their teaching staff and reduced teachers' salaries. The County was struggling, as was the nation.[22] The Depression dragged Americans to the depths of misery and was nearing rock bottom by late 1932. Thousands of banks had failed, more than 13 million people, one in four, had lost their jobs, and wages had plunged to 30 percent of their pre-depression level.[23]

9

Section 5

Birth of the CCC

In this time of despair, when fear and uncertainty reigned, Franklin D. Roosevelt, in his acceptance of the Democratic presidential nomination, stepped up to the plate. With courage and confidence, he declared "I pledge you, I pledge myself, to a new deal for the American people."[24]

County Goes Democratic First Time In History
Following the strong Democratic vote throughout the nation, Burnett county broke all precedents Tuesday and cast the first Democratic vote for a presidential candidate in its political history.
Journal of Burnett County November 10, 1932

Immediately following his inauguration on March 4th of 1933, he began to assure and engage the American people through his fireside chats. "I propose to create a Civilian Conservation Corps to be used in simple work. More important, however, than the material gains will be the moral and spiritual value of such work." The President's courage moved the nation to action. Working with a new Congress eager for bold change, FDR passed 15 major legislative innovations within a "Hundred Days" of taking office. The Civilian Conservation Corps, first known as Emergency Conservation Work, was established March 31, 1933.[25]

OFFICIAL PRESIDENTIAL BALLOT

Make a cross (X) or other mark in the square ☐ opposite the names of the candidates for whose electors you desire to vote. Vote in ONE square only.

FRANKLIN D. ROOSEVELT......President ⎫
                                     ⎬ Democrat ☐
JOHN N. GARNER..........Vice President ⎭

WM. D. UPSHAW................President ⎫
                                     ⎬ Prohibition ☐
FRANK S. REGAN..........Vice President ⎭

HERBERT HOOVER ....President ⎫
                                     ⎬ Republican ☐
CHARLES CURTIS ....Vice President ⎭

NORMAN THOMAS ....President ⎫
                                    ⎬ Socialist ☐
JAMES H. MAURER........Vice President ⎭

WM. Z. FOSTER................President ⎫
  (Communist Party)   ⎬ Independent ☐
JAMES W. FORD............Vice President ⎭
  (Communist Party)

VERNE L. REYNOLDS............President ⎫
  (Socialist Labor Party)   ⎬ Independent ☐
JOHN W. AIKEN............Vice President ⎭
  (Socialist Labor Party)

Section 5 - Birth of the CCC

Roosevelt's plan was to put unemployed youth to work in reforestation and other conservation projects across the country. The Army would run the camps and the Department of the Agriculture/Interior would be responsible for work projects. The Department of Labor would coordinate the selection of enrollees, but the Relief Administration in each state would make the actual selection.[26]

Not everyone was in favor of the CCC program. Conservative business interests, proponents of limited government, felt the program was destructive to private enterprise and individual initiative. Labor unions feared the lowering of the standard wage.[27] Environmentalists, such as Aldo Leopold, believed that CCC administrators did not appreciate the complexity of the environment and the optimum balance between wildlife and forests.[28] Others feared the CCC boys could be indoctrinated as the children in Hitler's youth camps were indoctrinated in Nazi ideology and basic military training.[29]

Franklin D. Roosevelt, a conservationist, established the Civilian Conservation Corps within one month of taking office.

Section 6

Enrollment

In spite of critics, within three months the CCC developed into the largest peacetime governmental labor force in American history. One thousand-four hundred and thirty-seven camps were selected, divided among eight Army Corps areas. The Sixth Corps Area (Illinois, Michigan and Wisconsin) received 139 camps, accommodating 27,000 men. Illinois received 33 camps, Michigan 59 camps, and Wisconsin 47 camps.[30]

The initial national call was for 250,000 boys[31] to be enrolled by July 1, 1933. Boys from every part of the country signed up. They came from cities and from farms, both the educated and the uneducated. There were five applicants for every opening.

Burnett County boys filed their applications with Chas. V. Blom, relief director located in Siren. Applicants were to be single, between the ages of 18 and 25, unemployed, and preferably from families receiving public aid. Each boy enrolled would receive a cash allowance of $30 per month, of which $25 would be sent home to assist his parents. They also would receive clothing, board and room, medical attention and entertainment.[32]

The enrollee was interviewed by the local selection agency to determine his capacity to benefit from the CCC. He then had a physical examination to conclude if he was fit for work and free of disease. To keep him free of disease, he received inoculations for typhoid fever and smallpox, and instructions in hygiene. A program of physical training prepared him for work in the woods and assessed his reaction to discipline.

Upon acceptance into the CCC, he took an oath of enrollment. He was expected to work a five-day 40-hour week and adhere to camp rules. The initial enlistment period was for six months, after which enrollees were given the option to reenlist for another six months. The length of stay varied, some being discharged at the end of six months while others stayed for several years. Boys could be released for good reason or dismissed for bad behavior.

33 of Unemployed County Residents to Spooner Tomorrow
Those passing physical examination leave tomorrow night for short preparatory training at Fort Sheridan. Thirty-three single men from Burnett County will go to Spooner tomorrow where they will undergo physical examinations for enrollment in the CCC. The men are instructed to meet at the National Guard armory at 1 PM. Three of the above are alternates; if any of the other 30 are rejected the other three will fill their places. Those accepted at Spooner will leave there tomorrow night for Fort Sheridan ILL where they will be given an intensive 10 day training to condition them for work in the woods. They will then be sent to the forests to engage in their planting activities.
Journal of Burnett County May 25, 1933

Section 6 - Enrollment

THE CCC — A YOUNG MAN'S OPPORTUNITY
to work
to live
to learn
to build
— and to conserve our National Resources

The 33 who will leave tomorrow are:

Lewis Jensen	William Revor
Howard Hitchcock	Clarence Trumble
Leslie Norine	Alvin Schultz
Alfton Anderson	Perry Clapsaddle
Ryland Anderson	George Millette
Richard Hunter	John Heier
Milton Westrom	Thomas Miller
Leslie Johnson	Robert Kaminski
Leonard Ortendahl	Kenneth Love
Joe Herzog	Stanley Adams
Norman Danielson	Arnold Larson
Edwin Johnson	Conrad Eklof
Elmer Buskirk	Ralph Wandby
Harry Goodell	Albert Baker
Harvey Springer	Myron Larson
Leon Davis	John E. Carlson
Raymond Hartshorn	

1939 CCC recruitment poster. Wisconsin Historical Society WHi 5762.

13

Section 7

Rookies

Burnett County was among the first to receive a CCC Camp. Company 626 S-53, known as Camp Riverside, was located in section 21 Swiss Township approximately six miles east of Danbury.

Riverside CCC Camp rookie, Norris Hoag.

Federal Forest Camp Established East of Danbury
Much excitement was caused in Danbury at 7:30 Sunday morning when the train arrived with 200 of the men who had enlisted in President Roosevelt's reforestation program. The train was well loaded with supplies and as soon as the men had left their coaches a large breakfast was prepared on the vacant lots north of the depot, the boys were lined up in army style and were given their rations of bacon, eggs and cereal. Six trucks hauled the 15 truckloads of supplies to the campsite after the meal. Many Danbury people witnessed the activity and army methods under which these men are handled. The work is mapped out for six months.
Journal of Burnett County, June 29, 1933

LeRoy Wells, one of the original recruits, described their arrival. "They plopped us down in the middle of the barrens and said, 'If you want a roof over your heads you better set up these tents.'"[33] The boys ate their meals out-of-doors and at night built a smoke smudge and placed cheesecloth over their bunks to keep the mosquitoes at bay.[34] The only structure built that spring by State Forest Rangers, Jim Devereaux and Clairemont Miller, was an office for H.T.J. Cramer, Forest Project Supervisor.[35] It would not be until August, two months later, that they would have a bathhouse.[36]

Camp life was far different from anything the enrollees had experienced. Many were away from home for the first time. To urban youths, the sudden transfer to the

Section 7 - Rookies

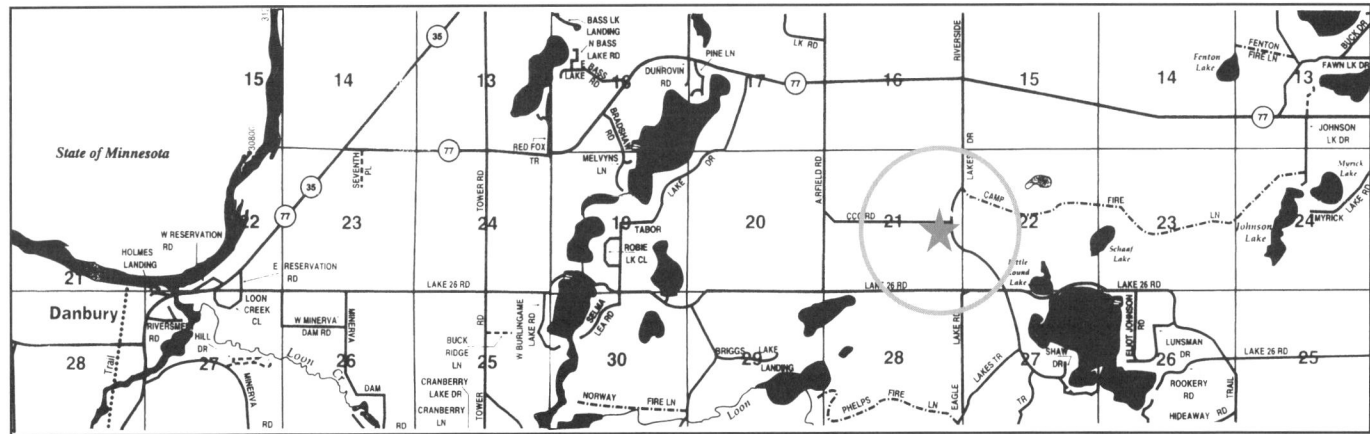

strange silent forests in a remote wilderness camp was a real cultural shock. For some, it was their first steady job, their first taste of hard manual work and their first encounter with regimentation and effective discipline.

Dear Sir   *November 20, 1933*

I am the only one in camp from Burnett County and my buddy is from Hayward. I was sent as a replacement two weeks after the quota from Burnett County went to the Fort (Fort Sheridan) so I was all alone and I did not know any one in the company that I was put in. However, it did not take long to get acquainted and I was soon treated as though I had come with the bunch. We landed in Westboro on my birthday, and I might remark that it was the most miserable birthday I have ever spent. We rode all night and arrived at the town of Westboro at five a.m. The town was just as I expected to see it a decayed logging town, which used to be in the center of a great white pine country. It now has a population of about two hundred. The size of the town was enough to depress the boys from Kenosha and Racine, but being used to a small town it didn't bother me. When we got to our campsite was when my courage got a severe shock and I almost regretted ever joining the CCC. An advance detail had come before us and I had it figured in my mind that they had the camp all ready for us, but when we arrived all they had done was to erect a fly for an out door kitchen.

We had a breakfast of cereal and scrambled eggs and immediately went to work clearing a camp site. Now we have our barracks up and it looks as though a miniature city has sprung up in a month and I am very glad I did not go "over the hill" during the first week. I remember that it seemed like a detention camp the first month but after that we started getting acquainted and taking in the dances and shows. We were given reduced rates on most things like that and our camp was pretty well behaved so people liked to have us come.

Most sincerely,
Dennis Gatten [37]

Camp Riverside was located six-miles east of Danbury, in section 21, Swiss Township.

The Power of Sand – Burnett County Civilian Conservation Corps

Riverside CCC Camp approaching from the south on Lake Drive.

A final step in a recruit's induction into CCC life was the test of a rookie's merit - initiation. New enrollees were fair game for the pranks and tricks of their more seasoned barracks companions. If you could come up smiling with a closed mouth, you earned the respect of every fellow in the company. Some could take it while others could not. "If you get in, you will either come out a man or a monkey" stated one enrollee.[38]

Memoirs of a Rookie
By Thomas Gordon

After a long period of anxious waiting, twenty-one young men of very doubtful appearance were enrolled as members of the CCC at Barron, Wisconsin. We arrived in Danbury on August 5th. We're met by the trucks at the train. A cold drizzle was coming down and we were not in the best frame of mind when the Chief Foreman said, "Park your baggage on one truck and climb into the other." Imagine our surprise when we found some nice hard benches to sit on in a bouncing truck. We were not given a chance to protest and we were herded into the trucks and taken to camp.

Initiation was bound to come, but before that we got our shots. Every man stretched the needle to such a state that the doctor would have to double it twice and stick it through my foot for the serum to reach my shoulder.

"All rookies out for guards." and guard we did until all the trees turned into goons and we decided that the goons could guard the camp better than we could. "Somebody come and get the cot stretcher, inspection tomorrow," was another command. Drizzel, the boy from Brill, hunted high and low but no cot stretcher could be found. Finally he was informed at headquarters that the cot was long enough.

Riverside Low Down, August 16, 1935
Riverside CCC Camp Newspaper

Section 7 - Rookies

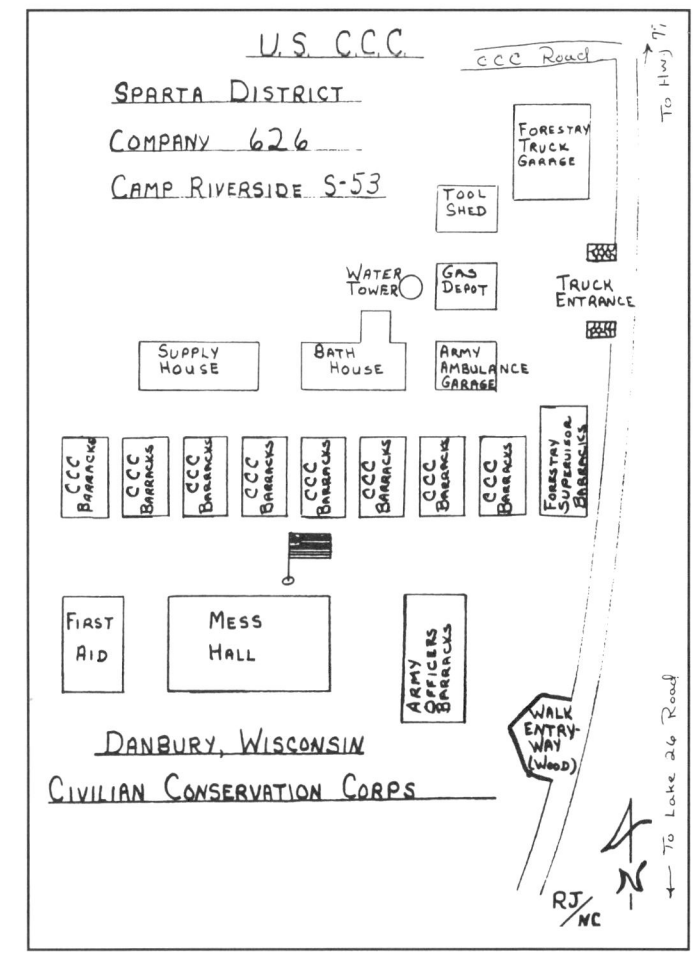

The Rookies
The coming of dawn was told by the skies
And from my bed I did arise
Put on my clothes and ate a lunch
And signed up with the rest of the bunch.

My nerves were shattered and completely shaken
For I had fears of not being taken
But when the doc said your okay
It surely was my lucky day.

We rode all day and half the night
And finally stopped at dawns early light.
Into a waiting truck we did pile
And greeted the Louie with a smile.

When we arrived at camp for mess
I felt homesick nevertheless.
Then to the supply house for our beds
And across them we all spread.

We layed around most the day
And some were undecided whether to stay.
But I had made up my mind to stay at last
And now the sorrowfull part is past.

Six months have flown by and I am still here
For 'tis home to me and very dear.
For it has taken many, many weeks
To build me up and tan my cheeks.

When the news goes around that
  rookies are to arrive
The camp is active as a bee hive.
Planning jokes and other things
Upon the rookies to spring.
   Popeye
   Riverside Low Down, April 24, 1936
   Riverside CCC Camp Newspaper

Schematic of Camp Riverside, as remembered by Roy Jarvis. **Below:** Riverside camp's fleet of trucks transport boys and supplies to and from work sites.

The Power of Sand – Burnett County Civilian Conservation Corps

The camp's large labor force made light work of winter snow storm clean ups.

Life in camp was just about what a fellow made of it. The first month was the hardest. The most common cause of dissatisfaction among new recruits was the idea that they knew what the score was. Most boys adapted well to their new life. In February 1934, nine months after the start of Camp Riverside, 74 percent of the boys signified their intention to reenlist for another six-month period.[39]

> *It seems the fellows from Joliet, Ill., can't take it. There are at present only 9 boys of the original 26 that are now in camp. We often wonder what those fellows would have done if they had been here last summer - without floors, electric lights or radio? How would they like fighting fires all day and night in hot windy weather with poor food to eat? It seems that the better conditions are the more grumbling.*
> *Riverside Low Down, June 21, 1935*

The boys lived in tents during the first summer of the camp. Winter quarters, however, were needed in September when CCC authorities decided Riverside Camp would continue to function throughout the winter months.

70 Men Employed in Building Winter Quarters At Danbury CCC Camp

Structures include barracks, mess hall, headquarters, and first aid building. Completion is expected in three weeks providing the present weather conditions prevail. Contract for construction was let to Fred Hall, Danbury, on October 9th, at which time he immediately started getting his lumber and supplies to the campsite.

The contract calls for the construction of 13 buildings. The winter quarters consist of six barracks, 20 feet wide by 112 long, and when completed will

Section 7 - Rookies

be lined inside and papered outside. Each one will house 38 men. The mess hall and kitchen will be 20x144 feet. Headquarters and office building 20x48 and first aid building 20x32 feet. A powerhouse 16x20 feet, which will hold gas engines and the electric light plant, a garage 20x40 and two smaller buildings 8x18 feet will complete the winter housing facilities.
Journal of Burnett County October 19, 1933

The camp buildings were not insulated. Tarpaper covered the outside, and in 1936 they added plywood to the inside of the barracks and mess hall to ward off the cold winter temperatures. Bert Lund described winter in the barracks. "Wind blew through the cracks in the walls. In the morning there'd be snow on your blankets. To keep warm, Jake Crandall went to bed with his overcoat on." Russell Stewart said, "You'd have to cup your hands to light a cigarette. After-shave lotion froze in the bottles." For heat, each barracks had two or three barrel stoves, with someone in each barracks assigned to keep the stoves going through the night. During the early years they burnt wood which the CCC crews had cut and split. Later years are described by Warren Melin. "They had two 'Warm Morning' stoves and a large cast iron inner casing to a furnace in which they burned coal. Sasse filled the large casing to the top with coal and when the lights were out at night, it glowed red."[40]

Boys from the South wondered what they were going to do when the temperature dropped to zero. They were kept mighty busy hauling wood when the temperature dropped to a minus 40 degrees. They gathered around the barrel stoves and kept each other warm with cold weather stories.[41]

The CCC boys cut and split the large wood supply that was required to heat the camp buildings during the exceptionally cold winter months of the 1930's.
Below: CCC boys used themselves to measure the snow depth.

CCC Boys arrive at a winter work site in cold, uncomfortable government trucks.
Below: CCC Boys awake and retire to the sound of Albert Gill's bugle.

Cold winter spells allowed a relaxation of the tight camp schedule. John Dunn stated, "We stayed in the barracks when it was 10 below." When the weather warmed, however, Retreat and Reveille were back in action. The bugler, Albert Gill,[42] blew reveille at 6 a.m. to awaken the boys, who no doubt, wanted to sleep a moment longer. They washed and dressed in their work clothes to attend 6:30 breakfast. Following breakfast, they policed the grounds and tidied their huts. A little attention in the morning meant a free evening. At 7:15, they formed rough platoons for roll call and inspection. After receiving their work assignment, they hung their number on the "Call Board" so they could be found if necessary. At 7:30 a.m., they climbed aboard the trucks and left for the day's work projects.[43]

Section 8

Conservation Projects

The project superintendent, employed by the forestry department, supervised all work projects away from camp and had eight to ten foremen under him. The foremen were usually "Local Experienced Men," L.E.M.[44] Forestry training was not required of either the superintendent or the L.E.M.[45]

More County Woodsmen Sent to Fort Sheridan
Herman and John Hinz, Siren; and Axel Olson, Daniels; were taken to Spooner last Friday and enrolled in the CCC as skilled woodsmen leaving that evening for Fort Sheridan, ILL. The above were selected from a group of six men who took the physical examination. This increases the number of Burnett County men, who have been classified as skilled woodsmen, to nine, six having been sent to camp the first of last week. They were Martin Murphy, Danbury; Art Hammer and James McCann, Meenon; Arthur Peterson, Siren; Fay Ketchel and George E. Hanson, Rusk. Journal of Burnett County June 15, 1933

Millard M. DeBow, Riverside Camp Project Superintendent from 1934 through 1942. **Right:** Alfred West, Foreman of Grantsburg side camp. **Below:** Riverside Camp Forestry Personnel, first row left to right: Donald Seeback, Wilfred Erickson. Second row left to right: Martin Johnston, William O'Gara, N.C. Dunn, M.M. DeBow.

21

Section 9

Forest Protection

Grantsburg side camp was located south of Highway 70 and west of the ranger station.

Fighting forest fires was the most urgent task of the CCC boys. The CCC added available manpower to the fire fighting efforts of Fire Protection District #2 to which Burnett County belonged. Within two minutes of receiving a call, they were in trucks and on their way.[46] To further increase the availability of the CCC boys, they established permanent side camps at Spooner and Grantsburg during the fire hazard seasons. A crew was also stationed at Webster for the same purpose.[47]

> ***Twenty-four boys are to be permanently stationed at Grantsburg.***
> *They started dynamiting and other operations Monday to clear about one half acre of land west of Andrew Pederson's and south of the fire tower, where they will pitch their three tents for living quarters and one mess tent.*
> *Journal of Burnett County, April 19, 1934*

The aim of fire-fighting efforts was to keep the fire from spreading by surrounding it with a plowed line or utilizing wet barriers such as marshes, rivers, and lakes to block the fire's progress. Firefighters with picks, shovels and water packs, which they carried on their backs, patrolled the line, putting out hot debris as it leaped over the plow line. Myron Dahl said the packs held five gallons of water and were heavy when you tried to run with them.

Section 9 – Forest Protection

Over 300 CCC Boys Battle Forest Fires In Anderson Town.

Three fires have been brought under control after threatening to destroy farm homes and battling against the efforts of between 300 and 400 fighters since Monday. One in section 17 started Monday morning and caused the greatest trouble, being at its worse Tuesday and yesterday when it traveled along a five-mile front. The entire force of fighters was concentrated on this blaze and it was only brought under control after covering a length of seven miles.

Another fire in the Fish Lake vicinity, near Art Shogren's gave considerable trouble by spreading in the peat and eating its way down into the bog where it smolders as a constant menace that may at any time give forth sparks to a carrying wind. The area was enclosed with a large ditch made by a caterpillar tractor and was under careful check until it jumped the ditching and started a new fire one mile further north. It was brought under control yesterday afternoon.

The largest fire, near Wood River, in the PB Brown neighborhood was under patrol Monday night. The Martin B. Christopherson farm was given up as lost by its occupants and they had household goods and cattle loaded on CCC trucks for a hasty departure but prompt and stubborn fighting saved the home from damage.

Nearly the entire CCC camp of 150 men from Riverside reported in addition to others from sub-camps at Spooner and Grantsburg. Volunteer residents from Spooner and Grantsburg swelled the ranks of fighters. All

CCC boys fight a fire with well-jetting equipment.
Below: A fire is fought by CCC boys carrying water packs on their backs.

23

The Power of Sand – Burnett County Civilian Conservation Corps

CCC boys jet a well in 15 minutes making available a fast water supply for fighting forest fires.

Spooner men returned yesterday afternoon leaving the Riverside and Grantsburg CCC boys to patrol the burned areas. The patrol will be continued until a heavy rain extinguishes any sparks that might lurk as a potential source of starting fires.
A peat bog fire on the meadow north of Grantsburg Sunday afternoon covered five acres in Sec 36, town of West Marshland. CCC fighters brought it under control by evening and it has since been patrolled under direction of Chas Nordstrom.
Journal of Burnett County May 3, 1934

In 1934 fires were contained to an average of 27 acres. But in 1936, drought conditions caused by high temperatures, winds and lack of rain created a tinderbox across the county. The soil had turned to dust and fires were nearly impossible to extinguish once they started. Using wet barriers was not effective as many of the creeks and swamps were dry. Crews were in constant readiness. By August 6, the Fire District had already fought 130 fires.

Riverside Camp was deserted as boys spent 12 to 48 hours at a time suppressing fires. Fighting fires in temperatures of 100 degrees, breathing smoke-stained air, catching little sleep, the tired, dirty, and hungry boys neared exhaustion. Ninety boys from the Highland and Platteville CCC camps came to their rescue. After 17 hours of travel, the boys arrived and were immediately thrown in as a relief unit on the front line. Most of these men had no experience as firefighters, but to the Riverside CCC boys they proved their worth.[48]

Grantsburg Fire

The fire at Grantsburg is demanding most of our attention. It is raging in a peat marsh covered with a heavy growth of hay. Two hundred men are kept on constant watch. Ditches three feet deep were dug around it but still it is impossible to stop it. The well jetting crew has pumped 387,000 gallons of water with little effect. George Shriever, Assistant Leader in charge of this crew has had only three hours of sleep in the past 72 hours and is still going strong. Two men were accidentally run over by a truck bringing in supplies as they were grabbing 40 winks. Neither was seriously injured. Many men have passed out from the intense heat.
Riverside Low Down, August 14, 1936

To make available a prompt and sufficient water supply for fighting forest fires, Geologist Harold J. Kundert, foreman of the Ground Water Survey Project, with his Camp Riverside crew surveyed the county's water table levels. They identified and mapped appropriate locations for wells. With this information and well jetting equipment, a well could be sunk within 15 minutes. The well water filled truck tanks, water cans carried on the

Section 9 – Forest Protection

backs of fire fighters, and hoses run through the woods. The most effective weapons for fighting forest fires, however, remained backfire, plowing and fighting by individual men.[49]

Early detection was a commanding factor in the ability to contain a forest fire. The windmill-type fire detection towers constructed by McDonald were dangerous as they could be toppled in high wind. Eighty-four foot steel towers, specifically designed to withstand wind, were replacing the windmill towers at the time the CCC arrived. The CCC continued these efforts and according to a 1937 news account had constructed four fire towers: the McKenzie tower and three others whose identity is unclear. In 1938 they replaced the Sterling tower.[50]

Manning the towers during fire-hazard season required many monotonous man-hours. The availability of CCC boys relieved local men and most likely increased the number of observation hours. According to the Riverside Low Down, two to three CCC boys, "stool pigeons," were stationed at the Danbury, Grantsburg, Siren and Spooner towers. The towers, 8-1/2 stories high, gave them a panoramic view of the countryside. In five-hour shifts, they scanned the horizon for smoke — and pondered. They slept in tents below the towers. Later they built cabins at the lookout sites.[51]

View of Grantsburg from the Grantsburg Fire Tower. **Below:** 1932 photo of the new Danbury Tower before the old fire tower was torn down.

Spooner Side Camp
Flocks of geese and ducks have been seen flying south, in their usual formation, reminding us of the approaching snow and cold, which we have braved so often. Tower men will soon pull stakes and leave their bird nests until next spring, when they will again go on duty.
Riverside Low Down, October 25, 1935

CCC crews harvest and set thousands of telephone poles connecting lookout towers with fire rangers.

When the tower observer spotted smoke, he phoned in his sighting. The single-line phone system established by McDonald was noisy and incompatible with commercial two-line systems. To improve communication, the CCC boys constructed a new two-line system throughout the fire protection district. Working in teams, CCC crews cleared trees and brush along the proposed line, harvested thousands of cedar logs for telephone poles, dug holes, set poles and strung the metallic telephone line. They built lines from the ranger station at Spooner to each lookout tower and to the homes of emergency fire wardens, from Spooner to Siren, Webster, Danbury and Grantsburg. One hundred and seven miles of telephone lines were completed.[52]

Once fires were located, men and equipment were dispatched to the site as quickly as possible. To facilitate access, the CCC boys created a network of roads through isolated areas and connected fire towers to main roads.[53] With the use of a caterpillar tractor, dump trucks, picks and shovels, they cut and cleared brush, pulled stumps, removed rocks, leveled slopes, filled in ruts and surfaced trails with gravel. Until they had their own dump trucks, they borrowed them from the Minong camp and worked in double shifts starting at 5:30 a.m.[54]

The trails were constructed 16 feet wide to allow the passage of a single truck. The trails connected Northern Burnett County to Northern Washburn County, Northern Burnett County to Douglas County, and Blaine Township to Webb Lake and Swiss Townships. Another truck trail was constructed along the Wisconsin/Minnesota border to prevent the spread of fires across the state line and to give access for fighting fires.[55] With minimal equipment and maximum effort, the CCC boys constructed approximately 75 miles of truck trails. One enrollee proudly commented. "This road is so well done it is mistaken for County Trunk H by traveling tourists and salesmen." County Trunk H is currently Hwy. 77.[56]

Section 9 – Forest Protection

Once the trails were constructed, they needed to be maintained. Keeping trails clear of debris decreased the fire hazard and facilitated the use of roads and trails as fire breaks. Brush from trail construction and roadside maintenance was burned during the winter months when it could be done with greater safety. Roy Nordquist said he enjoyed working with heavy equipment. He drove a cat for road grading, plowed for tree planting and maintained the trucks.

Some trails necessitated the building of bridges. The Camp Riverside boys constructed three small vehicle bridges, two over Loon Creek and one over Rock Creek.[57] The CCC highlight in bridge building was the 130-foot, two-span timber bridge over the St. Croix River on St Croix Trail in Blaine Township. The boys logged 100,000 board feet of Norway and white pine for the bridge and auxiliary projects. After the timbers were sawed, they built a foundation at the mill and framed and fitted the bridge completely before moving the timbers to the bridge site. When the timbers were moved to the river, they set up a creosote plant and placed the timbers in a large vat of heated creosote. Using log framework and support timbers, they constructed substantial abutments on either side of the river and a central pier and then filled them with rocks. In less than

Gravel is shoveled onto trucks for road surfacing. **Inset**: CCC boys who came to the camp from cities learned to use cross cut saws and axes to blaze trails. **Below:** The start of a 16 foot wide trail.

27

The Power of Sand – Burnett County Civilian Conservation Corps

Bridge built by the CCC boys over the St. Croix River in eastern Blaine Township. **Below:** A road grader was used for road preparation and maintenance.

a month's time the bridge was moved out over the water, the timbers put in place, and the bridge was made ready for use.[58] The following year, to conform to engineering requirements, a 1/4-mile long guardrail was added and the bridge raised 3-1/2 inches.[59]

Ranger Maley and his crew are devoting their time and energy to bridge construction work. The bridge they are working on will afford transportation over Rocky Brook (Rock Creek) in Douglas County and connect the Big McGraw Lake Road in Burnett County with County truck T in Douglas County. It will be worth your while boys, to go up and look over this and get a smattering of what Mr. Maley is teaching his boys in the art of bridge construction.
Riverside Low Down, August 30, 1935

Section 10

Buildings and Park Construction

Other CCC construction projects included a log sub-station garage at Webb Lake and a solid brick Ranger Station at Webster.[60] The Webster Station included a five-stall garage, an office with maple floors, and an upper area for sleeping and storage. Constructed in 1935, it took six weeks to build at a material cost of $1,500. If built by conventional carpenters, the estimated cost would have been an additional $3,000.[61]

The Grantsburg Ranger Station, constructed by the Works Progress Administration (WPA), was completed two years later in 1937. Assisting with the construction, the CCC hauled gravel and built a sewerage system for the ranger station and connected it with the Grantsburg system.[62]

The CCC sawed over 100,000 cedar shingles to be used in state park camp construction and developed recreational parks at Riverside, Clam Narrows, Clam Dam and on the Clam River at the present Meenon park site. Ranger Alfred West and CCC foreman Warren Melin supervised the Meenon park pavilion construction. CCC boys quarried the slate rock used in the construction from a pit in northern East Blaine Township.[63]

Meenon County Park pavilion under construction. **Below:** A 1980's photo of the Webster ranger station built by the CCC in 1935.

29

Section 11

Forest Development

The primary focus of the Riverside CCC Camp was forest development. As the county acquired land for forests, they needed to identify their land boundaries. Early surveyors divided the county into one-mile square sections. At each section corner they placed a wooden marker or marked a tree, which was known as a bearing tree. Because of the cutting of bearing trees and the rotting of the original wooden corner posts, the area required re-surveying. Bob Baker and Ben Connor, with two CCC crews, surveyed over 76,000 acres of county land. Permanent metal posts with heavy brass caps were positioned at each section corner. John Dunn, a member of Wilfred Erickson's mapping & survey crew, described the process. "To find section corner markers, we used a WWI issue compass, a tally wacker, and survey chains. A tally wacker was a counter worn on the finger and was used to count steps. For me 26 steps equaled one chain. There were 80 chains to a mile. A lot of the work was done in the winter time wearing snowshoes."[64]

The forest development plan, which spread over a six-year period, was to plant 2,500,000 jack, Norway, white pine and spruce trees across the denuded county lands. The first task of the Riverside CCC, young inexperienced boys from Chicago, was to clear recent fire debris from 1,500 acres in preparation for planting. Planting involved scalping the area, which is the removal of all vegetation from a two-foot-square spot where a seedling is to be planted. They averaged about 500 scalps per man per day, which amounted to about twenty acres per day. Each spring and fall the camp received their seedling allotments. In the fall of 1933, they planted their first plantation, 90,000 red pine. Norris Hoag said he "planted 1,250 trees in one day using a spud." Tree planting reports vary depending on the source. CCC records report 400 acres with nearly half a million jack and Norway pine were planted by 1939, with another 400 acres ready to be planted. County Forest records report from 1,603 acres with 2,212,155 trees planted by 1940.[65]

Planting of 200,000 trees to Start Tuesday
Keith Stafford, our mechanic, and one of our truck drivers left Wednesday noon for Wisconsin Rapids to get 100,000 Norway pine. From there they will go to Front Lake to pick up 100,000 Jack pine and will arrive here Friday afternoon with 200,000 trees for the boys who will begin to plant Tuesday afternoon, the day after Labor Day. Rangers Johnston and Guest will probably have charge of the planting, which will be about two hundred acres in area. We have received one new, long wheel base state truck, which will be a considerable help in transporting the men to and from the field.
Riverside Low Down, August 30, 1935

Section 11 – Forest Development

The first plantations did not do well. Lack of a nurse crop cover, soil cooked by fire, poor planting techniques, lack of moisture and probably time of year the trees were planted all supported a crop failure. The camp superintendent and foremen were not familiar with forestry techniques and did not receive the training to adequately supervise planting procedures. The severe weather of 1936 baked the young trees, killing all but those planted in areas sheltered from the scorching sun. The average temperature was close to 90 degrees for the entire month of July, and rainfall was only slightly over 1/4-inch. Acres of dead trees from one to two feet high stood as memorials of the summer of 1936. Following the loss of so many trees, efforts were made to improve planting methods. The camp received instructions in proper planting techniques and cool root cellars were constructed to protect seedling before planting.[66]

CCC boys clearing land in preparation for tree planting.

Our fall planting program is now in progress.
500,000 Jack and Norway pines are being planted on lands that had previously been planted, but due to the drought were unable to survive. Two crews of twenty-two men are averaging 1100 trees daily per man. All the planting will be done in furrows over approximately 416 acres of the old planting grounds. Dead trees are cleaned from the furrows by dragging a log over them.
Riverside Low Down, September 11 & 25, 1936

CCC boys planting trees. By 1940 over 2,200,000 trees were planted in the county.

Trees by Joy Killer

I hope that I shall never see,
Another bucketful of trees.
They make my poor old head go round,
And keep my nose right to the ground.
My back is broke, my legs are dead,
Oh, what I'd give for a good soft bed.
But the foreman says NO - forge ahead;
Sometimes he makes me see quite red.
Trees are made by God it seems,
But only a CCC would plant the things.
By D.B.
Riverside Low Down, September 25, 1936

Trees were procured from state nurseries at Wisconsin Rapids, Trout Lake and Gordon. To assist the nurseries in obtaining seeds for planting, the CCC boys gathered bushels of pine cones at the appropriate maturing time for each species. By 1937, they had collected 6,600 bushels of tree seed. The Riverside CCC boys also tried their hand at the nursery business. They planted jack pine seeds in 20 nursery beds near the camp. Each bed contained about 1,200 trees, which would be ready to plant in two years.[67]

In winter the boys improved the forest stand by release cutting of suppressed trees, which decreased competition with the healthier trees. Duane Sandberg worked on the TSI (timber stand improvement) project. "We lined up and walked through the tree planting, cutting down dead and bad trees." By 1936, the boys had completed 2,320 acres of forest-stand improvement on Burnett County forestlands. They also inventoried forest cover, and by 1937, had completed 115,000 acres.[68]

Another project undertaken by the CCC to protect the forests was the control of blister rust. Blister rust is a fungus disease destructive to white pine. Wind-borne spores from infected pines are spread to the leaves of raspberry and gooseberry bushes and then back again to the pines. Since the disease cannot spread from pine to pine, ridding the area of raspberry and gooseberry bushes (genus Ribes) was thought to effectively control the disease. The CCC crew systematically scoured the woods, pulling out by hand thousands of these bushes.[69]

Section 12

Lake and Stream Improvement

Although their principal goal was reforestation, they also worked to nullify the ill effects of logging on lakes and streams. Cutting trees along rivers removed the natural shade that maintained the cool temperature of water necessary for the spawning of fish. Spring log drives also gouged and scoured the riverbeds, further damaging the natural habitat of fish.[70]

During winter months, the Riverside CCC boys built brush refuges, pole tangles, spawning boxes and spawning stars to enhance the habitat for fish. Boxes, built three-foot square and filled with gravel, provided spawning places for bass. Refuges, complex masses of brush woven together in six intricate layers, provided breeding places for aquatic life, food and shelter for the smaller fish, which in turn were fed upon by the larger fish. A completed refuge, a 6 x 6 x 16-foot structure, required eight to ten sandbags to weight it down in 8-10 feet of water.[71] The fish refuges were moved over the ice where they were sunk through holes cut in the ice with an ice saw. Yellow, Viola, Devils, Dunn, Minerva, Des Moines, Webb, Warner, Sucker and Big Bear lakes all benefited from these habitats. To this day these refuge areas are considered good fishing locations.[72]

Below: CCC boys build brush tangles to improve fish habitat. Inset: Brush tangles are pulled out over the ice and sunk.

The Power of Sand – Burnett County Civilian Conservation Corps

Weighted sandbags were used to sink the brush tangles. **Below:** CCC boys construct spawning boxes which were placed in the rivers and lakes of the county.

Refuges, spawning boxes, log tangles, and spawning stars
Piles and piles of them stacked up at the different lakes on which we are working. We certainly hope the fish appreciate our kindness in providing food and shelter. During the past week the boys experienced a thrill in watching the sinking of refuges, log tangles, and also a few of our power horses, Rangers O'Gara, Lawson, and Rueter. If it hadn't been for a few of the boys, we sure would have had a few odd-looking fish in the Des Moines Lake.
Riverside Low Down, December 13, 1935

34

Section 12 – Lake and Stream Improvement

To further aid stream improvement, CCC crews built deflectors and bank covers. A deflector, a winged structure of logs or stone, speeds up the current of the river. The faster current increases the oxygen content of the water and washes away the sand from the deeper gravel layer of the river, creating deep holes. All are necessary for trout to flourish. A bank cover is a mass of poplar poles nailed to form a mat about three feet wide, which provides shade to keep the water temperature from becoming too warm. By July 1936, the CCC had constructed 135 bank covers along the Clam River.[73]

CCC boys from the Grantsburg side camp worked at the Osceola Fish Hatchery while boys from the Riverside Camp worked at the Spooner Hatchery. They cleaned fish ponds of fungus growth, vegetation and sediment matter. They jetted a well for the Spooner Hatchery[74] and planted 95 cans of brook trout from the Osceola Hatchery in the surrounding creeks.[75] They netted fish in small landlocked lakes and transferred them to larger lakes, which were nearly sterile.[76]

A new problem regarding county lakes came to the forefront in 1934. The lake levels were dropping at a dramatic rate. A State Conservation Commission meeting was held at Webster to address the issue. Jess Perry reported that the shoreline on Sand Lake had decreased by 300 feet in the last five years. Another Sand Lake observer said its depth had dropped 37 inches in the past four years. A Viola Lake resident said his shoreline had receded 18 feet last year and that the present water line is 80 feet from its normal point,

CCC boys cleaning tanks at the Osceola fish hatchery.

CCC boys constructing a drainage ditch near Warner Lake to raise the lake's water level.

reducing his shoreline from 3,500 feet to 300 feet. Devils Lake was reported to have receded five to six feet in the past seven years. Chas. Mahlen, a summer resort owner on Lake Minerva, recommended the building of dams to raise the water level on the 26 Lake chain.[77]

Ralph Immel, chairman of the conservation commission, explained the cause of the lowered lake levels. "The shortage of rainfall over the previous four years and the impact of settlement were behind the problem." He urged residents to "stop draining the peat bogs and marshes and to stop cutting tree coverage. That is the long-time remedy for drought."[78]

Several dam construction projects were proposed to raise lake-levels. They called for dams to be built on Loon Creek, Clam Lake, Webb Lake, Loon Lake and on the Yellow River in either Rusk or Sand Lake Township.[79]

The CCC constructed a large earthen dam on Loon Creek to raise the water level on the Loon Creek Chain of Lakes.[80] To raise the water level on Warner Lake, they dug a ditch and created an earthen dike to divert the previously natural drainage of a three-mile swamp from Pokegema Lake to Warner Lake. The first year following the project, Warner Lake rose five feet.[81]

The WPA constructed a dam across Loon Lake in 1937, raising the water levels in Loon, Cadotte and Shoal lakes.[82] In 1939 plans were underway to construct a dam at the outlet of Webb Lake to maintain its water levels.[83]

To monitor lake-levels, the CCC lake survey and mapping crew constructed and established bench mark monuments. They also created lake maps, which included

Section 12 – Lake and Stream Improvement

Warner Lake water levels rose 5 feet following the CCC drainage project. **Below:** Lakes were surveyed during the winter. Snowshoes were often worn.

descriptions of swamps, weed beds, dams, inlets, outlets, length of shoreline, areas of sand and muck etc. and shore development such as dwellings, resorts, cover type and roads.[84] Norris Hoag and Duane Sandberg members of the lake survey and mapping crew, describe the survey process. "Lake surveys were done in the winter. Using a transit, the lake surface was sectioned off into a 100-foot grid. We drilled a hole through the ice at each section corner and dropped a marked chain to determine lake-depth. At the end of the chain was a cup with a valve used to retrieve soil samples." Mr. Hoag remembered surveying Little Yellow, Devils, the 26 Chain (but not Lake 26) and Big Sand lakes.

Section 13

Wildlife Management

Logging and forest fires not only affected lakes and streams, but also the natural breeding places of birds and animals. The CCC boys fostered the restoration of wildlife by taking deer censuses,[85] isolating game refuges,[86] raising pheasants and building birdhouses.[87] In February 1938, the CCC boys counted 132 deer in drives conducted in five county townships: Blaine, Swiss, Webb Lake, Union, and West Marshland.[88]

> ***Sixty-four deer reported seen on 800 acres.***
> *Census shows deer still plentiful in section. 64 deer were reported seen on Dec 12 when approximately 800 acres were covered by ninety-four men who were taking a deer census in the town of East Blaine. In taking the census men are placed on all boundaries of this area. The "checkers" on three sides are stationed far enough apart to be able to see the man on his right, and count the deer that pass between them. On the fourth side the "drivers" are spaced 100 feet apart and drive the deer ahead of them until they have all left the area. This is the first time a deer check has ever been held in this section of the country so the approximate percentage of deer killed during hunting season can not be estimated.*
> *Riverside Low Down December, 16,1936*

The CCC surveyed two proposed game-refuges, No Man's Refuge in the town of Blaine and Spruce River Refuge in the town of Dairyland. No Man's Refuge covered 3,000 acres, the Spruce River Refuge 5,660 acres. Leader Ben Connor and enrollee Stanley Nary marked their boundaries while CCC crews brushed a 12-foot-wide swath to enclose each refuge. The boys experienced tough going in the Spruce River country as they worked their way through burnt timber and heavy underbrush, the results of a forest fire the year before. After clearing the refuge boundaries, the CCC placed 150 metal signs, eleven to the mile on standard posts set four to five feet above the ground. The signs "Wisconsin Wildlife Refuge No Hunting or Trapping, Conservation Commission" warned hunters of the refuges.

Working with the Burnett County Conservation Association, the CCC boys raised about 3,000 pheasants from chicks to sturdy game birds and released them throughout the county. Warren Melin recalled the birds dying like flies. Because of his farm experience he realized they had "white diarrhea" and suggested they purchase Potassium Permanganate from the Danbury Pharmacy. The birds survived and from then on during the summers he raised pheasants and chucker partridge.[89] They also cut dry cedar for the construction of birdhouses. Martin, wren, and swallow houses were distributed to state parks, ranger stations, and hatcheries throughout Northwestern Wisconsin.

Community Service

Section 14

Although the primary purpose of the CCC was the restoration of the county's natural resources, they were always ready to assist others in time of need. During the drought of the 1930's, farm fields were inundated with grasshoppers. Each year as the drought increased, the grasshopper hatch increased. In 1936, the most serious damage was on the Chester Isack farm in Dewey Township.[90] The CCC boys were called upon to spread poisonous bran over the entire farm.[91]

Sparta District CCC trucks lined up and ready for flood relief work.

> On June 26th a squad of men were detailed to aid a farmer in a fight with the grasshoppers. 10 sacks of poison were spread. This poison, being composed of a mixture of sawdust, bran, and molasses, was spread over 200 acres by the boys. It was distributed as you would sow any grain. The insects were plentiful in spots and mowed down oats to the ground. An early start seems to have checked the progress of the hoppers for the time being at least. It is estimated that approximately 2 million of the insects were killed. Riverside Low down, July 10. 1936

The following year the hatch spread across Dewey and LaFollette Townships,[92] and by 1938 it was across the county. Three poison-mixing stations, D'Jock's Mill in Siren, Billiet garage in Grantsburg and Ed Swan's farm in Roosevelt Township, provided poison bait to

Flooding along the Mississippi near Arkansas.

farmers. The CCC boys mixed and sacked at the Siren station, WPA workers at the other two. Sodium arsenite poison was mixed with sawdust and whey at the rate of 55 tons per day. "In some places where the bait has been applied, the dead grasshoppers are so numerous that they can be shoveled."[93] Each summer the poison was mixed and spread until the drought scourge ended.

The county sheriff also called upon the CCC boys for assistance. Under the supervision of Sheriff George Iverson, they dragged lakes for drowning victims and covered miles of territory in search of lost individuals.[94]

In 1937, when the Ohio and Mississippi rivers overran their banks forcing 500,000 people from their homes, the CCC offered their services. The Sparta District furnished 450 of their best trucks. Nine hundred officers, cooks, senior foremen, leaders and truck drivers, including men from Camp Riverside, assembled at Camp McCoy. After being organized into battalions and equipped with supplies, they rushed to Illinois, Missouri, and Arkansas to assist in the relief. Enrollees built sandbag dikes up and down the rivers, and helped rescue and evacuate thousands of flood victims.[95]

Section 15

Riverside Camp Life

Food, clothing, shelter, health and education were under the direction of the Army. The Army's Sixth Corps (Wisconsin, Illinois, and Michigan) consisted of five districts and eight sub-districts. Sparta was the district headquarters for the Riverside Camp, Pattison was the sub-district headquarters. Care of Camp Riverside's 200 men was under the charge of the camp commander. To assist him he had a junior officer, camp doctor and educational advisor. Routine and discipline, facilitated by an array of Army regulations and regular inspections, was the glue that held the system together. The Index to the Rules Book was 120 pages and covered everything, from abbreviations to vaccinations, from china and glassware breakage, to notification of relatives of enrollee illness. Area, district and sub-district inspectors checked and rechecked administration efficiency and camp safety.[96] Routine inspections were held each evening at 5 p.m. The grounds were inspected, personnel were inspected, and the barracks were inspected. Awards were given for military courtesy, for the neatest and cleanest barracks, and for the best-dressed man. Even the camp collie inspected the men.[97]

In addition to regulation, there was regimentation. The standard daily routine was 6 a.m. reveille, 6:30 breakfast, 7:15 roll call and 7:30 off to work. A 30-minute noon lunch break was taken at the work site. An inspection report states: "I have seen them 'dinnering-out' when the temperature was below zero and their spirits were the best."[98] Warren Melin recalls noon lunch. "They placed a 10 gallon milk can filled with water and coffee grounds

Eating lunch at the work site.

41

The Power of Sand – Burnett County Civilian Conservation Corps

CCC boys holding their mess-kits waiting for lunch at the work site.

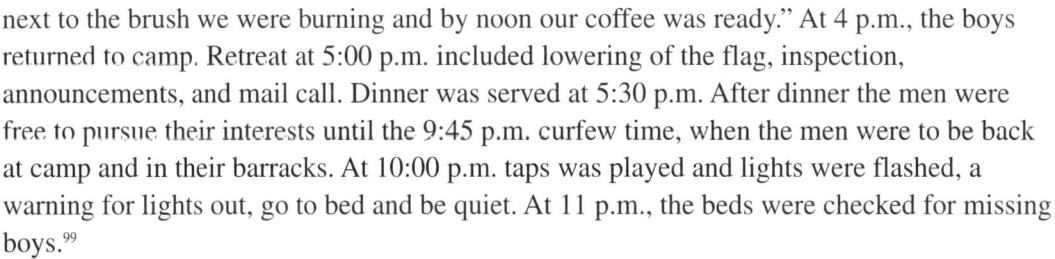

next to the brush we were burning and by noon our coffee was ready." At 4 p.m., the boys returned to camp. Retreat at 5:00 p.m. included lowering of the flag, inspection, announcements, and mail call. Dinner was served at 5:30 p.m. After dinner the men were free to pursue their interests until the 9:45 p.m. curfew time, when the men were to be back at camp and in their barracks. At 10:00 p.m. taps was played and lights were flashed, a warning for lights out, go to bed and be quiet. At 11 p.m., the beds were checked for missing boys.[99]

Regulations and regimentation fostered camp pride. Improvements to the camp, new construction, remodeling, and beautification, were on going, with nearly all the work done by the enrollees. Two five foot high slab-rock posts on either side of the truck entrance tapered down gradually over eight feet to blend in with a wall of slab-rock set on end. On the uppermost part of the gateposts, small spruce trees grew in hollowed out cedar posts.[100] White birch arbors marked the visitors' entrance to the camp.

Within the camp, white guideposts with black tops edged the concrete sidewalks, and light posts located at the corner of each building lit the night sky. Spruce trees bordered the company's main street. Sod filled the space between the barracks. Lilac and iris procured from an abandoned homestead, dispersed color and fragrance. Window boxes of hollowed-out cedar logs graced the forestry building. An arch, rock garden, fishpond and flagpole were located in front of the mess hall.[101]

Signs helped rookies and visitors find their way around the various camp buildings;[102] headquarters, officers' quarters, forestry quarters, warehouse, blacksmith shop, carpentry shop, truck garage, educational building, kitchen/mess hall, dispensary, seven barracks, bathhouse, latrine, and pump and electric building with its Kohler engines.[103]

They moved the forestry supply building and mess hall to make room for a larger garage for new trucks. They built an addition to the garage for a blacksmith shop and repair shop.[104] They remodeled the old oil house into an office, dividing it into two rooms, one for Army and one for Forestry. The two rooms had separate entrances, "so as not to interfere

Section 15 – Riverside Camp Life

Cozy quarters of the CCC barracks. **Below:** Typical barracks ready for inspection.

with each other's work." This arrangement must not have worked, because several months later, plans were underway to construct an Army office in the south end of barracks #3. The original Army headquarters was remodeled for living quarters for the officers and an educational adviser.[105]

The whole company was enthusiastic over the planning of a larger and better reading and recreation room. The furniture; chairs, floor lamps, bookshelves, end tables, smoking stands, magazine racks, and settees, was constructed by the enrollees. The old wallboard was covered with veneer paneling. Covering the west end with oak slab logs, inserting a window in the center and extending the roof edge outward gave the entrance to the reading room a neat log cabin appearance.[106] Bryon

Visitor's entrance to Camp Riverside.

Baker recalls the library. "It was really nice. The walls were covered with pealed pine logs, stained and varnish. It was real pretty."

In August 1936, just a couple months after receiving new hardwood floors and a sterilizer, the mess hall burned. According to the camp paper, ladders were placed and a bucket brigade formed in less time than it took to tell it. Although the entire kitchen was badly scorched and part of the food spoiled, it did not stop the kitchen force from putting out breakfast the next morning. Later repairs to the mess hall included partitioning off one end for the officers' mess.[107] On occasion remodeling required the expertise of skilled men. Mr. Lorentsen and Mr. Bueholz came from Sparta to remodel the shower house. The completely renovated bath included a new roof, (tar) paper on the outside walls, a cement floor, new sinks with both hot and cold faucets and a 100-gallon hot water boiler. The new shower house was painted black and white, as were the dispensary, canteen, kitchen and barracks.[108] Byron Baker recalls "We'd take a shower as hot as we could get it, and then we'd run and jump into a snow bank. It was probably a dare."

Living conditions at the Grantsburg side camp also improved. During fire season the men slept in tents and ate their meals outdoors. In 1935 they built a mess hall, and in 1936 they constructed a barracks from lumber they obtained by wrecking old buildings. The boys logged jack pine which was split to finish the inside, giving it a log cabin effect. The barracks were not quite complete when a storm that almost floated them away, tents and all,

Photo of Camp Riverside taken from the water tower. **Below:** Forestry building at Camp Riverside.

Section 15 – Riverside Camp Life

forced the boys to move inside. "If any of you fellows have TB you should be here. We have the original open-air barracks," wrote an enrollee from the Grantsburg side camp to fellows in the main camp at Riverside.[109]

Camp life also fostered pride in personal appearance. Each enrollee received two sets of clothing, pants, shirts, jacket and shoes. They did their own laundry by hand. Some industrious enrollees set themselves up in business. "Your laundry work done for $1.00 a month, O.D.'s cleaned and pressed $.25, extra shirts $.15, civilian clothes extra. See George Jolley." "Suits or overcoats tailored to fit you for $16 and $20. See Harry Kamka, barracks #2."[110] Myron Dahl recalls his business. "I ironed shirts for 10 cents. They had to have a crease in each shoulder, and a crease down each side front and back. I used a flat iron heated on the barrel stove. The money paid for my cigarettes." Myron also remembered cutting off the end of his blanket to insert in the seam of his trousers to make bell-bottom slacks "We liked the Navy look. I was caught and had to pay for my blanket and scrub floors for punishment."

At the Camp Canteen the boys could buy pop, candy, cigarettes, and toiletries. The proceeds were used for recreational activities. Cigarettes were about 10 cents a pack, but you could buy papers and a 1# can of "Prince Albert" tobacco and roll your own cigarettes.[111]

Camp Riverside barracks. **Right:** Photo of Camp Riverside taken from the roof of barracks #7. **Below:** New barracks at Grantsburg side camp.

45

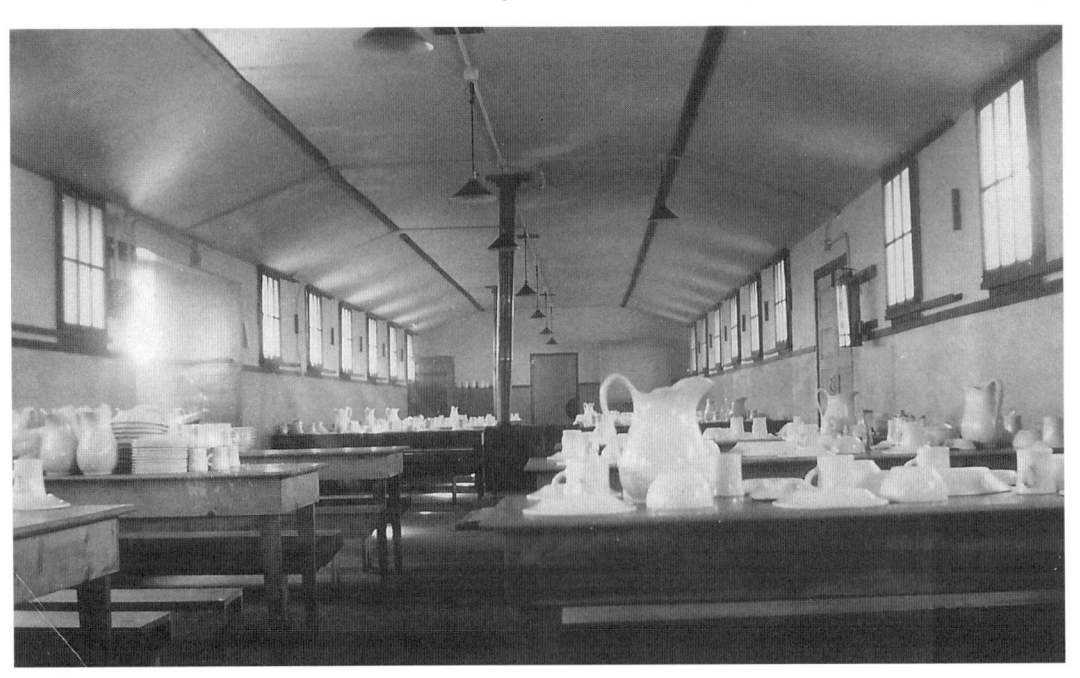

CCC camp mess-hall. The average ration was 33 cents to 46 cents per day.[116]

> *Dear Folkes:*
>
> *Well how is every body down home.*
>
> *I feel prity good I got a touth pooled yesterday it didn't cost me a sent. I'm going to get one fild next time the dentist comes. Boy we have fun up here. Last night I was over to the next barex playing games they tiped every bed over and caryed them from one end to the other. Saturday night I bought a $3.50 ring for 10 cents for a sovener. Boy we sure get plenty to eat my belt don't even fit me any more. One felow out of the seven of use was sent back becose he had one finger of on his right hand and his other was all cut up form a shot gun shell. They even took ouer finger prints. They ishsed use one pair of pants, 2 shirts, too overal pants, 2 overal jakets, 6 pair sox, 1 pair overshous, 2 shous, 1 pair logers and 4 coats. We get ouer pay day the 31th if we sighn the pay roal. We don't have to get up till 8 o'clock in the morning. We go to work at half past nine and work till eleven, then we got to work at 2 and work till a qarter to 4 then we poot on our good close for retreat. This camp is half made up of Indians and negrose. Boy them negrose can sew. One is pooting the belt on my uniform. There is a little raidio in our barex and It's going all the time. One of the Pink boys came in our bunch and to others from Bedlianger that I know. All you can see up here is sand and Pine trees about 12 ft. high. There's lotse of wild duckes, sqerls and deer up here theres three lakes within a mile frome our camp. All the officers are pritynice exsept one of the formers. Gee the time gose fast. It seems as if I was hear only one day, I'm going to get my picut taken the ferst good day, Well I'll have to quite know, right soon.*
>
> *Riverside Low Down December 13, 1935*

Section 15 – Riverside Camp Life

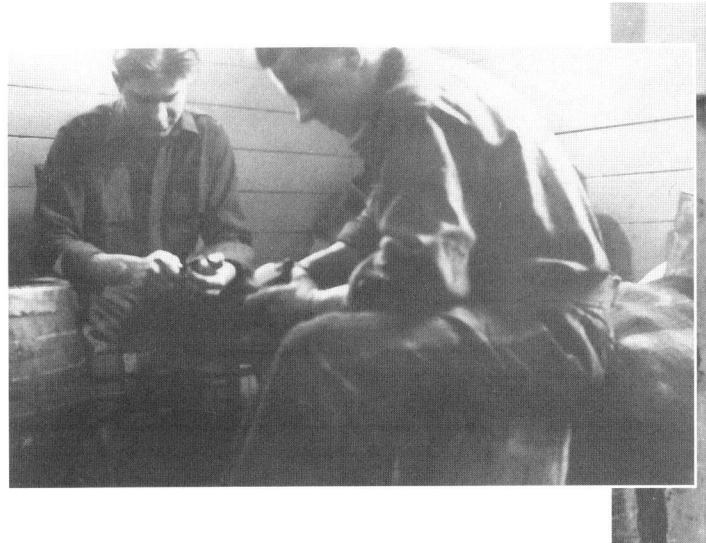

Dress slacks and shirts (OD's) were to be worn during mess. They were to be quiet while they ate and were not to smoke in the mess hall. The way to a man's heart is through his stomach would definitely apply to a CCC camp. The need for cooks in CCC Camps was featured in enlistment notices in April and May 1935.[112] The food for the most part was nutritious but bland. Most of Camp Riverside's inspection reports listed the food as fair to good. The Riverside Camp superintendents recommended good lumberjack cooks as their top priority, and the elimination of the Army as their second priority. Four months after making their recommendations, the food was still not considered up to par, and the superintendents arranged to have their own mess.[113]

Russell Stewart and Bert Lund said, "Cockroaches were everywhere. They were in the sugar bowl and in other food stuff." Bert Lund and Ivol Paulus commented, "The food was nothing to write home about, until a cook transferred in from another camp. Then the food was good." Johnson and Rylander were the two cooks most often mentioned.

Special meals were prepared for holidays. The entrees were gleaned from the regular ration allotments occurring before and after the holiday, which if gleaned too quickly resulted in meager meals.[114] In spite of the poor rating of the food, it was nourishing enough. Most of the boys upon entering the CCC were underweight and undernourished. Food and physical labor added an average of 7-12 pounds to each enrollee. The health record among CCC men was much better than the health reports from cities and towns in the United States. Warren Melin recalls a boy named Sasse. "He was barely five foot four inches, but he could really put down the food. By the time he left the CCC he was over six foot with wide shoulders. I wonder when he returned home if the folks even knew who he was."[115]

The boys received regular physical exams, inoculations, and instructions in hygiene. The spread of communicable diseases was always a concern. In May 1936 the camp was quarantined for scarlet fever.[117] Most health issues were what might be expected for young men, hernia, appendicitis and physical injuries.[118] When they required treatment, they were sent to the Grantsburg or Fort Sheridan hospitals.

After a days work in the field, the boys were selected for their rotation through KP. **Right:** CCC Camp cook. A good cook meant a happy camp.

Camp Riverside ambulance in front of infirmary.

Lawrence Davis writes from Base Hospital.
Each patient receives a pair of pajamas at least two sizes too big and a bathrobe and slippers that fall off continually until he learns to walk in them. After he is given a bed in the ward he goes to work if he is able. He has to be pretty bad before he is unable. There are two ward nurses to take care of 50 or 60 patients, so some work has to be done by the patients able to get around.
Riverside Low Down, September 25, 1936

Four deaths occurred at Riverside Camp, two from illness and two from accidents. Bert Lund remembers trying to arouse Jerome Schneider for reveille. "We were ready to head out the door for breakfast but Schneider was still in bed. I went to get him up, but he wouldn't wake up."

Jerome Schneider is Mourned by All in Camp
Jerome Schneider age 18 an enrollee of Camp Riverside, died Monday morning November 2, at the Grantsburg Hospital from diabetes mellitus, contributor, respiratory failure. The deceased was born at Independence, Wisconsin on September 5, 1918 where he spent his life until enrolling in the CCC. He is survived by his mother, Agnes Schneider, and five brothers and sisters.[119]
Riverside Low Down, November 6, 1936

Leonard Smith, age 19, died at the Grantsburg Community Hospital after a short illness. He had been an enrollee at the Riverside Camp for six months. Pallbearers were six friends from the CCC Camp at Menomonie.[120] Stanley Tamulonis, age 18, and George Conrad Ulbricht, age 21, drowned May 30, 1935, in Lake 26 when their boat containing a party of five capsized. Other members of the party were rescued by camp youths that saw the tragedy from shore. There was to be no swimming until further orders. On June 13, Dave Brown and Ted Ryczek left for lifeguard school.[121]

Section 16

Education

The Army was responsible for the welfare of the boys beyond their current camp experience. One of the mandates of the CCC was vocational training and educational instruction to prepare enrollees for employment after discharge. The training provided, however, was not an apprenticeship for any specific trade. Vocational classes generally related to the enrollee's camp assignment, enhancing his skill and appreciation of the projects on which he worked. The enrollee's work and camp experiences were as valuable to him as the classes he completed. Potential employers knew that a man with CCC experience was a man who knew discipline, hard work, and how to get along with others.[122] Ivol Paulus said he left the CCC for a job at the Webster Creamery for $100 a month. "It seemed like a lot, but later I realized there was no clothing, food, rent or health care. All these had been provided in the CCC." Roy Nordquist said he was out of the CCC for awhile, but when he couldn't find work, he re-enlisted.

With education and experience an enrollee could advance within the CCC by becoming "rated." These men helped with the operation of the camp and forestry projects as leaders, assistant leaders, supply clerks, cooks, educational assistant and physician assistant. Rated men were paid $36 and $45 a month compared to $30 per month for the average enrollee.[123]

CCC boys at map work.

CCC boys were proud of Camp Riverside's library and reading room.

Classes were offered in the evening and in the morning hours before the boys left for work. The educational advisor, camp officers, physician, technical staff and the enrollees taught the classes. The educational level of the men at Camp Riverside in 1934 was higher than the average CCC camp. Most of them had at least two years of High School, several had graduated, and some had attended universities.[124] For those who had dropped out of school, Camp Riverside offered classes for the completion of the eighth grade.[125] Many took advantage of the opportunity. Twenty-one men from Camp Riverside received their diplomas in 1939-1940.[126]

Riverside Camp Eighth Grade Graduates
Charles E. Krebs, Franklin M. Moritz, Ronald E. Smith, Orville J. Marks, Clifford E. Olson, Ralph V. Day, George W. Borg Jr., Steve Clementi, Veronne G. Wischer, Fred Peterson, Eugene A. Freeland, Alfred Songetay, Edwin C. Songetay, Blaine B. Manor, Gilbert Brown, Marvin E. Roatch, Martin Y. Johnson, Alex Rosio, Elmer R. Goodenough, LaVerne E. Willims, Morgan O. Knutson.

Educational Classes Offered at Camp Riverside
Academic: Civics, Economics, English, General Science, Geography, German, Mathematics, Physics, Spelling, and Writing.
Vocational: Art, Auto Mechanics, Blasting, Bookkeeping, Carpentry, Cooking and Baking, Engineering Practices, Fish and Game Management, First Aid, General Forestry, Geology, Journalism, Leather Work, Leader and Foreman Training, Life Saving, Map and Map Making, Mechanical Drawing, Mess Management, Photography and Photo Development, Radio, Shorthand, Sign and Poster Painting, Surveying, Telegraphy, Telephone Line Construction, Typing, Welding, Wood Carving and Wood Working.[127]

The camp had a library, which contained a selection of books designed to assist with employment after discharge. *Careers*, *The Profession of Forestry*, and *Job Hunting and Getting*, described a variety of jobs and what an individual needed to do to fill a chosen position. Many books dealt directly with specific vocations and occupations, providing enrollees with a chance to investigate possible careers.[128] The library also contained over 200 books of light fiction, detective and western stories, to induce the men to spend their leisure time with their noses in a book. In addition, the Riverside Camp received the benefits of two traveling libraries that moved from camp to camp.[129]

> *The enrollees of Riverside camp take this means of expressing their appreciation of the reading material that Mrs. Maser of the Webster Drug Store has been furnishing them with. Mrs. Maser for the past two years has been saving the back issues of all the popular magazines, and at the end of each month she lays them aside and makes it an obligation of hers to see that the boys at Riverside have something to read during their leasure hours.*
> Riverside Low Down, September 13, 1935

Some classes provided the enrollee with experiences beyond his specific corps assignment. The camp newspaper, *The Riverside Low Down* was printed the second and fourth Fridays of the each month by the camp journalism class. Through the paper, the enrollees developed skills in interviewing, writing, typing, drawing, advertising, production and printing. In 1936, *The Riverside Low Down* received a four-star rating, an accomplishment the class was very proud of. The best compliment for the newspaper staff, however, was the request to continue to receive the paper by those being discharged.[130]

A radio class was taught by Mr. Osterheld, the camp's educational adviser. Using old transmission and receiving equipment, they assembled a broadcasting unit in the educational adviser's office and installed loudspeakers in each barracks. The system broadcast daily class schedules and other announcements. Besides the mechanics of radio construction and operation, the boys also had the chance to become radio artists on the regular Saturday CCC radio hour WEBC in Superior.[131]

> **Our Boys Pinch Hitted for Camp Delta**
> *Camp Delta was supposed to give a radio broadcast but couldn't because the camp was quarantined. The program was a wow even tho they had only a little time in which to get ready for it.*
> Riverside Low Down, May 10, 1936

Some educational experiences involved trips away from the camp to see specific vocations in operation. Trips included: the U.S. Naval Training Station in Duluth, the Superior Evening Telegram and Broadcasting Station, the Wood Conservation Plant and Paper Mills of Superior, the Agricultural Experimental Farm in Spooner. To see the use of various tools they visited the Kell-How-Thompson Hardware Co.[132]

Section 17

Sports – Recreation – Leisure

Sports, as participant or spectator, were available to enrollees during their leisure time. Dr. Waters, the camp physician, procured a boxing ring and taught the boys the art of pugilism.[133]

CCC boys relaxing on the beach at Lake 26.

Riverside Camp Features Entertainment Program
Tuesday evening January 23, the boys from the conservation camp participated in a bit of lively sports consisting of wrestling and boxing directed by Lt. Geo. Frieder. The personnel and every member of Co. 626 attended the four bouts and two wrestling matches and all seemed well pleased with the show, each and every moment of the bouts were full of action and all carried on in a very sportsmanlike manner.
Journal of Burnett County February 1, 1934

Lt. James Sturman taught the proper sighting and mechanical action of guns and marksmanship. Enrollee Francis Tharaldson imparted the finesse of table tennis and billiards. In summer, they swam at Lake 26 where they had constructed a diving board. In winter, they skated on an ice rink across from the camp.[134] Basketball and baseball were the two most frequently reported sports activities. The Webster School Board offered the high school gym to the camp for basketball practice.[135]

52

Section 17 – Sports - Recreation - Leisure

Mr. Osterheld, Educational Adviser and James Pavlinec, team manager attended a basketball coaching school at Superior State Teachers College. Fine points of play, passing, guarding, floor work and different plays were discussed and demonstrated by the Minnesota team and the Superior Yellowjackets. First aid for common injuries was also instructed.
Riverside Low Down, December 16, 1936

They perfected their skills competing against each other, forestry against army, rookie against experienced man, and barracks against barracks. They competed in baseball and basketball, in pool and archery, in billiards and Ping-Pong, in wrestling and boxing, in spelling and in cards. They competed against other CCC camps and participated in local baseball and basketball leagues.

Forestry defeats Army
The forestry pick up team took the Army overhead team to camp by the score of 0 to 3. The Army still insists that they can beat a team consisting of only the forestry overhead.
Riverside Low Down, April 1936

On June 30, 1936, the seven CCC Camps in the sub-district held a field day at Superior. Approximately 1,200 men took over the city. After exhibiting their float, "The Progress of the CCC," in the morning parade, they competed in track and field, a tug of war and a pie-eating contest. Shumate of Riverside Camp took several awards in track and field, and Riverside won the tug of war competition over Camp Pigeon. "They competed not as rivals but as brothers, to see who was the most able in brawn and skill."[136]

This comradeship is of special interest because Riverside was an integrated camp, not the norm for CCC Camps across the country.[137] The mix of cultural backgrounds, educated and uneducated, farm lads and city boys, men of African American, American Indian, Polish, Irish, Hispanic, Italian, and Scandinavian heritage, all lived and worked together in a cooperative community. Living and working together, they learned they were often more alike than they were different, resulting in the elimination of many traditional prejudices based on ignorance and misinformation. Nevertheless, with the walloping amount of time spent together, personalities were bound to clash.

Barracks baseball game.
Below: CCC camp baseball players.

53

CCC boys of varied ethnic backgrounds.

It seems as though Molly and Mueller are on the outs. Well, fellows the grudge fight, which you two boys had, was surely fine example of clever boxing.
Riverside Low Down, October 15, 1936

Many evening hours were spent with their buddies visiting, playing cards and listening to the radio. The boys evolved a language all their own[138] and probably knew each other better by their assigned nicknames than by their given names. Byron Baker said they carved their names into their buddies' footlockers. Clarence Johnson and Otto Aubert debated the question, "Who can sling the most sarcastic remarks, a city slicker or a Wisconsin farmer?" They also struggled over the question of who was the greasiest, the dump truck drivers or the KPs.[139] No doubt they debated livelier unpublished subjects. The boys from one barracks chipped in and bought a radio, after which the whole company gathered there.

Spooner Side Camp
We have set up the stove in our barracks and the boys surely enjoy spending their evenings reading, playing cards and listening to the radio.
Riverside Low Down, August 30, 1935

Lights out came at 10 p.m. when talking stopped and the boys settled in for the sleep that only comes after a hard day of physical labor in the fresh air. They listened to the steady rain on the roof and knew that tomorrow the roads would not be dusty.[140]

Section 17 – Sports - Recreation - Leisure

The fellows in Barracks one are mighty glad, at times to have lights out at night. Fellows that are bashful raise their voice in music and fellows who have harmonicas bring them out to play.
Riverside Low Down, September 11, 1936

The talent and vast amount of tomfoolery in camp provided spellbinding entertainment. Drama classes by Mr. Osterheld, and singing classes by Mrs. Ida Jefferies, music teacher at Webster High, added confidence and style to their antics. There is no fun quite as enjoyable as that created spontaneously by your comrades.[141]

Amateur Night October 23rd
On Monday night of next week all entertainers of this company will have a chance to do their stuff. An amateur night will be staged in Barracks #7. A reward of $5 will be given to the one awarded first place. A free ticket to the movie will be issued to all participants who don't get the gong.
Riverside Low Down, October 11, 1935

Riverside barracks pals. Boys are unknown except for Alfred Kulbeck upper left photo, stooping, third from left.

The Power of Sand – Burnett County Civilian Conservation Corps

Boys, who wanted to sleep late on their day off, may be carried to the parade ground, bed and all, by their barracks comrades.

Sometimes the boys invited the community to events. To celebrate the completion of the camp buildings, they sponsored a dance with music furnished by the Ted Hunter orchestra, with between 400 and 500 in attendance.[142] On another occasion officers and a truckload of men joined the large crowd at a dance sponsored by the Grantsburg Side Camp, with music by the Aces of Rhythm.[143] The camp also invited the community to their weekly Friday night feature movie. The Journal of Burnett County estimated a crowd of 300 attended the show, *Guilty As Hell*, and the dance that followed.[144]

Sometimes they left camp riding in "recreational" trucks for social outings. Although the CCC boys were not allowed to have cars while in camp, the woods were full of them. With a car, local boys could go home on weekends. Ivol Paulus described his car experience. "I purchased a car, and while driving from my home in Oakland Township to Riverside Camp, I had seven flat tires. I could have walked it faster." For the most part, the camp officers over looked the transgression, especially if they were receiving rides to town.[145] Roy Nordquist explained that a camp commander found his car, and gave him sufficient grief, that Roy left the CCC.

The boys liked to travel to town, Grantsburg, Dairyland, Spooner, Webster. Favorite spots included Hog Wallow (currently Oak Grove), The Bloody Bucket (on Hwy 77 west of Danbury), the Siren Roller Derby (located on the north side of Main Street between First and Hanson Ave.), Danbury Town Hall, Merle Engels Place (located at junction of 35 and 77), and Log Gables.[146] They had girls on their minds. Bert Lund met his future wife at Hog Wallow. Friends went home with friends, where they met and married their sisters. John Dunn befriended Byron Baker and later became his brother-in-law. Pete Erickson took Albert Gill home to meet his sister Virginia. They also married. Some Riverside recruits from outside Burnett County, married local girls and chose to remain in or return to the area. Among them are Albert Gill, John Quigley, Garlen Ziehme, Jay King, and LeRoy Wells. Others married local girls and moved away.

The camp paper enjoyed reporting on the latest camp crushes. Beatrice Olson said the girls would not give their real names for fear of being talked about in camp. Someone reported to

Section 17 – Sports - Recreation - Leisure

the Riverside Low Down that Molly gave his last dime to a poor hungry girl who was just dying for a hamburger, and went hungry himself.[147] For the most part, the boys were well behaved and accepted by the community. A 1934 inspection report stated: "There was one riot in Webster last summer but the boys were not so much to blame as the bootleggers and local people."[148]

Attended Duluth Superior Football Game
It was a cold night and fifty miles in a government truck is no easy ride at any time but to good football fans these things are practically unnoticeable.
Riverside Low Down, October 16, 1936

Transportation was provided each Sunday morning for the boys who wanted to attend church. Sometimes local ministers conducted services at the camp. Reverend K.C. Myers of Webster brought the Peterson trio of Atlas with him when he visited the camp. The service was short, and the music was great.[149] Trips home for holidays and vacations before re-enrollment provided a reprieve from camp life.

Leave Provisions, Holidays and Weekends
About 116 boys from CCC 626 left Friday for Chicago to spend Sunday and Labor Day with relatives. Two special coaches were chartered from the Soo Line. The boys returned here for work Tuesday afternoon.
Journal of Burnett County, September 7, 1933

May I have this dance?
Below: Cars stashed in the woods.

57

Section 18

Benefits

Indian housing at Sand Lake.

Benefits of the CCC both for Burnett County and the CCC boys were immediate and long range, economic and personal. The CCC brought increased revenue to the county, and built a forest industry where agriculture had failed. It provided opportunities and hope for young men where none existed. Of all the relief programs developed during the depression era, the CCC was considered the most successful.

Immediate economic impact to the county came from CCC allotment checks to families on relief, hiring of local experienced men, the local purchase of camp supplies, and the patronization of small businesses by the CCC boys. The county averaged 72 enrollees per month during 1938. Each of the 72 enrollee sent home $25 per month which amounts to $21,600 for the year.[150] In addition to the hiring of Burnett County men for technical staff in CCC Camps, Camp Riverside hired local men for temporary jobs at the Danbury camp.

Approximately $2,500 was spent each month for food. Staple supplies were purchased in bulk through the district headquarters, while perishables and immediate needs were purchased locally. Consolidated Lumber in Webster, Babcock's Garage in Marksville, and Burnett County Oil in Danbury are a few of the local businesses that benefited. Businesses from Duluth/Superior that gained from the camp included: Elliott Co. Packers of Beef and Pork, Leamon-Bamby Bakeries, and Helland-Day-Erickson Wholesale Dealers in fruits and vegetables.[151]

Section 18 – Benefits

Local stores, jewelry shops, taverns and cafes advertised in the Riverside Low Down to attract the boys' spending money. Collectively each month the boys' pockets held nearly $1,000.[152]

The economic value of the camp's forestry projects cannot be separated from the efforts of those who came before and after the CCC. The WPA-Danbury Indian Village purchased the first timber, jack pine, from Burnett County forests in 1938 to build houses in the village. Ten houses were built at Danbury and another 18 at Sand Lake. Nearly 50 years passed before the first trees planted by the CCC were harvested. The 80-acre harvest sold for $10,666.40, $5.68 per cord in 1981 when it was thinned, and $11.16 per cord in 1986 when it was clear-cut.[153]

Riverside enrollee. Boys are unknown throughout the rest of the chapter except for Andrew Myers upper left photo sitting on the ground far left.

59

The Power of Sand – Burnett County Civilian Conservation Corps

The CCC not only assisted with the development of a county forest but also with the development of a conservation attitude. Camp Riverside held annual conservation tours of their projects to inform the community of their value and to educate the population to the importance of conservation.[154] School children toured the Riverside Camp and enrollees taught children how to plant trees in the first county school forest in May 1939.[155] They held tree-planting demonstrations throughout the county.[156] Other groups such as farmers through the

Section 18 – Benefits

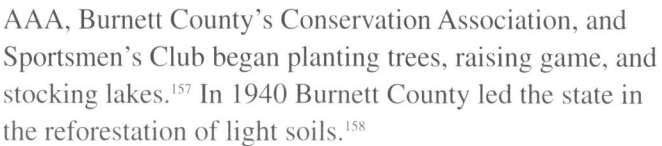

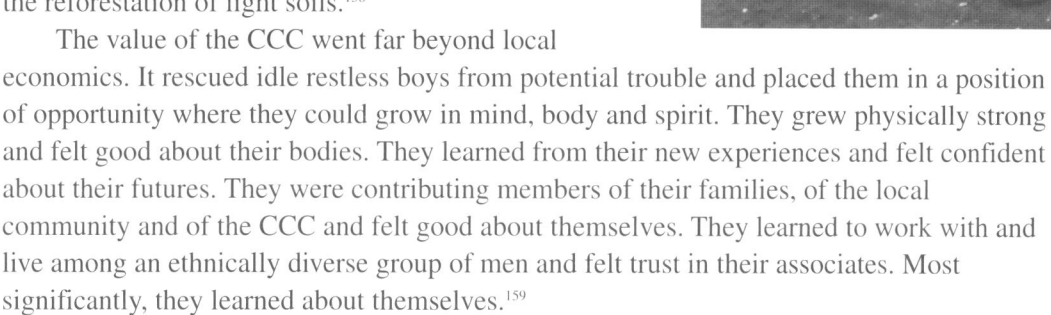

AAA, Burnett County's Conservation Association, and Sportsmen's Club began planting trees, raising game, and stocking lakes.[157] In 1940 Burnett County led the state in the reforestation of light soils.[158]

The value of the CCC went far beyond local economics. It rescued idle restless boys from potential trouble and placed them in a position of opportunity where they could grow in mind, body and spirit. They grew physically strong and felt good about their bodies. They learned from their new experiences and felt confident about their futures. They were contributing members of their families, of the local community and of the CCC and felt good about themselves. They learned to work with and live among an ethnically diverse group of men and felt trust in their associates. Most significantly, they learned about themselves.[159]

By narrowing the distance between the boys and their natural roots, they learned a lesson not taught in books but by the experience itself. They saw the beauty of the land and

The Power of Sand – Burnett County Civilian Conservation Corps

knew intrinsically they were of this beauty, not less nor greater than any other being. They affirmed their place in the universe and grew in strength, spiritual health and wisdom. Norris Hoag vouched for the CCC. "It was a good place to be," he said. John Dunn said, "It was wonderful. I needed something to do. I enjoyed it. Wilfred Erickson was my crew chief. He shaped my life more than any other person including my parents." Andrew Myers liked the fact that he worked at the camp. It made him proud to think that at such a young age, he could help his family during the depression. Affirming the value of their CCC experience, the CCC Alumni wished that young people today could have the same opportunity. Yet they realize, times are not the same today as they were in the 30's.

It would be hard for us to even begin to realize what we of the CCC would be today if it weren't for the effort and sacrifice that this great man (President Roosevelt) has put forth in our behalf. Most of us would still be idle with only a picture of a dark wall ahead and resentment in our hearts.
Riverside Low Down, January 30, 1936

Section 19

John Quigley and the CCC

The story of John Quigley reflects the impact the CCC had on the individual man. John's story, like the story of so many other CCC boys, is presented here, so that the subtle yet significant influences of the CCC can be appreciated.

John Francis Quigley was born February 21, 1914 to Francis and Iona Quigley in Chicago, Ill., the older of their two sons. John attended 2-1/2 years of high school and earned his Eagle Scout award.

Having been unemployed since March, John Quigley applied for the CCC at the Dupage County Emergency Relief Center in Glen Ellyn, Ill., on October 1, 1934. His physical examination at the time of his entrance into the CCC showed he was 65-1/2 inches tall and weighed 130 pounds. He received inoculations for typhoid-paratyphoid and smallpox. He listed his occupational preferences as mechanic and truck driver. Quigley enlisted with a neighbor, but a trick of fate sent them to different camps. After taking his oath of enrollment on October 20, 1934, John was sent to Camp Riverside.

John Quigley described the shock of his arrival at the CCC camp in Danbury in 1934. "After a 450 mile, 24 hour long train ride from Chicago, I emerged from the train blinking. You think you're at the end of the world," he recalled with wry humor. "You take all these guys out of the city and stick them in the woods, some go right over the hill."[160]

John Francis Quigley, Riverside Camp enrollee 1934-1937.

The first year at Riverside Camp, John strung phone lines near Viola Lake during the summer and built fish refuges in the winter. He recalled the extreme temperatures of the 30's. One evening, the driver of the truck that picked up Quigley and this crew brought blankets to keep the men warm as they road back to camp from Spooner where they were working. None of the trucks at the camp had heaters. The actual temperature was 52 degrees below zero.[161]

John took first aid and map reading classes. Most importantly he attended truck driving school and auto mechanics classes for which he received the highest rating. He served as a truck driver and later as mechanic. He became a rated man and helped

63

John Quigley and Helen DeRousseau.

conduct the driving school.[162] From January 29, to February 26, 1937 John was on Flood Relief duty in Blyville, Arkansas assisting the evacuation of flood victims. John was described as pleasant and reserved and stated he would remain in the CCC until the horse and wagon returned. He enjoyed photography and took many photos of camp life.

While working out of the Spooner side camp, John attended a barn dance at Highcamp's farm. It was here that he met Helen DeRousseau. Helen described their first meeting. "He was the truck driver for the CCC. The girl who got to ride in the front seat got the driver. I got the front seat."

At the end of September 1937, John declined to reenroll. His physical examination upon discharge showed he had gained eight pounds during his CCC enrollment. John returned to Illinois and was employed as a mechanic by various trucking firms for the remainder of his working days.

Helen joined him in Illinois, and they were married August 28, 1938. John and Helen had 12 children. John constructed miniature fish tangles for his children and told them of his experiences in the CCC. In 1954, he brought his family back to the area to spend their summer vacations on the Amsterdam Slough near Siren. In August 1962, they purchased a home on Old 35 west of Webster and in 1974 they retired there. He enjoyed hunting and fishing and making toys and banks with his woodworking skills.

John never forgot his experience in the CCC. He joined the National Association of CCC Alumni, kept his CCC Annual, photo albums and supported conservation efforts and the development of the Wisconsin Conservation Corps (WCC), a 1984 revival of the 1930's CCC. He and six of his Camp Riverside buddies maintained contact throughout their lives. John Quigley died December 4, 2001, at the age of 87, and is buried at St. John's Catholic Cemetery, Webster.[163]

Section 20

The Final Years

In spite of the economic benefits and the intrinsic value of the CCC, its stability was never certain. Designed as a relief program, its necessity and consequently its funding were always in question. In 1935, when the CCC was on the rise, Burnett County requested additional camps.[164] In 1937, President Roosevelt commended the CCC for their valuable work and recommended it have a permanent place in American life. He knew, however, that it would need to be reduced in size because of its drain on the treasury.[165]

In September, 1937, Riverside Camp, (one of the largest work areas in the state) received word that it would be one of the eleven camps in Wisconsin to be disbanded by the end of the month and that the boys would be transferred to other camps. County residents protested to the state headquarters with success. Riverside Camp would be one of 49 camps that would remain open. The CCC camp at St. Croix Falls State Park and [166] the Minong CCC Camp, a camp created through the division of the Riverside Camp in 1935, were closed. Both the Minong and the St. Croix Falls CCC boys were transferred to Riverside, bringing the camp's enrollee numbers to over 200.[167]

> More than 75,200 men from Wisconsin were enrolled in the CCC and more than 92,000 men served in the state. An average of 54 camps a year was operated with a total financial obligation within the state of more than $96,5000,000.[168]

Struggling through the trials of the final years, Riverside Camp remained open to the last days of the CCC. A decline in the quality of enrollees and camp leadership and the change of focus from conservation to military, damaged what had been a valid undertaking.[169]

The number of corpsmen enlisting in the CCC decreased, although in Burnett County there was always a waiting list. War plant recruitment, military enlistment, and the National Youth Administration (NYA) gave able men other options for work besides the CCC. To encourage outside employment, the pay in the CCC was lower than the standard wage, although still higher than relief. Enrollment notices changed from listing the criteria and the process of application to touting the advantages of joining the CCC.[170]

Earlier enrollment procedures allowed experienced men to re-enroll and allowed men up to the age of 29 to join the CCC. In the later years, to bolster a decreasing enrollment, the age requirement was lowered to 17-23, and the need to be on relief was dropped. The age limits were not always honored, and boys under the age limit were often accepted. Enrollment times, which had been every six months, changed to accepting applications at any time, with enrollees applying directly to the camp. These practices resulted in diminishing the quality of recruits entering the CCC. New enrollees were less committed, more easily discouraged, and more quickly overcome with homesickness.[171]

News from Riverside CCC Camp at Danbury, Wis.
Thirty-seven men will be leaving end of the month, 23 due to the restriction on time spent in the CCC and 14 from choice. This group is not as large as the group that went out in March. There are very few old timers left now and the groups can't be so big any more. A lot of key men are leaving with this group and many understudies are now busy learning the tricks of the trade.
Journal of Burnett County June 15, 1939

The decrease in the quality of recruits was accentuated by a decrease in the quality of camp leadership. The European situation caused the Army to drain the camps of their best officers, placing them into regular service. Their replacements had neither the character nor the experience to prevent a deterioration of camp morale and conditions.[172]

There had always been friction between the Army and Forestry departments, departments made of two very different types of people. The Army, which needed regulations to keep large operations running efficiently, used forms, procedures and regimentation. Forestry, on the other hand, consisted of outdoor men who understood the fluidity of nature and worked accordingly. Not necessarily appreciating the role each played, they rivaled for control.

I have had the privilege and honor of knowing RD Baker (Forestry) for over 19 months and to the present date I can't recall anything above a verbal encounter. He always seems to be a little skeptical as to whether or not the Army has any purpose or legitimate excuse for existing, but in spite of this evident shortcoming I think he's a hell of a good guy and a square shooter.
Lt. Ansel (Army)
Riverside Low Down April 1936

There is an unsatisfactory condition existing here (Camp Riverside) that reflects poorly on the present CC (Conservation Commission) and bids well to wreck the cooperation between himself (Mr. DeBow, Project Superintendent Forestry) and the(Riverside Camp) Superintendent (Army). It also has the enrollees' morale destroyed to a considerable degree. Already several of our key men have left, while others are now away seeking employment. We have lost the blacksmith, the survey leader, the type mapper, several truck drivers, and the two best tractor operators are away seeking other employment. I talked to our carpenter who is also about ready to quit. DeBow feels he will soon be entirely cleaned out of his key men. The whole trouble hinges on the small item of what the men should wear in the field.[173]

The decline in the character of CCC leadership, deterioration in the quality of recruits, and the subsequent loss of morale affected the quality of work. A letter from Fred Evert, agricultural agent for Burnett County, and a 1939 Danbury Fire Investigation Report reflected the issue:

Section 20 – The Final Years

Dear George,   *July 5, 1938*
The grasshoppers are the worst in history. Putting out a lot of poison. A car load, 60 barrels, poison coming to Siren today. The hoppers are getting worse and today the CCC crew didn't show up at all. I am mad enough to choke somebody. I guess they didn't get back after the 4th.
Fred[174]

The 1939 Danbury Fire Report did not represent the best-coordinated efforts of the CCC and local rangers. The CCC leadership failed to have a standby crew on duty at the camp on a day of high fire danger. The standby CCC man had practically no supervisory experience and 50 percent of the CCC enrollees were new men with no fire fighting experience. Some of the CCC leaders and some of the boys were unclear as to what was expected of them and failed to do what they were told. Other CCC boys were observed throwing stones into Loon Creek while other CCC firefighters were desperately trying to contain a fire that was crowning in the jack pine. This less than ideal performance did not rest solely with the CCC. The ability of local rangers to communicate instructions was also in question.[175]

The inability to appreciate the value of conservation, as well as the increasing threat of war in Europe, kept the issue of military training in CCC camps on the front line. Fear of military service discouraged young men from joining the CCC, although the boys in Camp Riverside did not fear being drafted.[176]

Militarism and the CCC
The virtues of the CCC have been mentioned often enough. It needs to be remembered, however, that the whole project could be robbed of most of the usefulness if the militarists succeeded in getting their hands on it. Maj.-Gen. George Van Horn Mosely commander of the Fourth Corps area suggests that the CCC be expanded to take in every 18 year old boy in the United States, and that it add military training to its curriculum. Such expansion of course would amount to conscription and would give us a cross between Hitler's compulsory labor camps and the universal draft feature of European military service laws. It is hard to see why the country needs either of these things. As things stand, we have a great asset in the CCC. We cannot afford to reduce its value by adding features that would be repugnant to American traditions.
The Superior Evening Telegram
Reprinted in Riverside Low Down, September 25, 1936

CCC Youth Not Trained For War Say Officials
The conflict in Europe had brought questions as to whether the CCC might be pressed into a role similar to the youth movement in Germany. The CCC offers assurance that enrollment in the corps would not entail military service. We want every mother in America to know that if her son is among the accepted October volunteers, he will not be put behind a gun. The CCC can not be inducted into the army service of the United States.
Journal of Burnett County November 30, 1939.

67

The CCC was a natural for military training as the boys were already familiar with Army routine and discipline. An amendment to the 1940-1941 relief appropriations measure provided for specialized training through the CCC in fields important to the Army. Byron Baker, John Dunn, Russell Stewart, Warren Melin and Roy Nordquist all stated the CCC helped them with their military experience. "Defense Training at Camp Riverside Getting Underway" read the headline of a May 29, 1941, article in the Journal of Burnett County. Fifteen hours weekly were devoted to classes in military support services if the enrollee desired to learn those vocations. Warren Melin recalls the Navy recruiting at the camp. Thus the focus of the CCC was being diverted from conservation toward fulfilling the needs of national defense.[177]

Following Pearl Harbor any federal project not directly associated with the war effort was in trouble. Congress, against the wishes of President Roosevelt, discontinued funding the CCC in June of 1942.[178] Camp Pattison closed in March 1942, transferring 43 corpsmen to Camp Delta at Bayfield and 67 to Riverside Camp. These were the only two camps remaining in Northern Wisconsin.[179] Those camps, which provided fire protection services, were the last ones to close. The local newspapers, caught up in reporting the war in Europe, made no mention of the closing of Camp Riverside. The Camp buildings were sold at auction May 8, 1954.

Many years after the closing of the camp, Andrew Myers visited the abandoned site. He walked around the area and commented, "You'd never know that such an important event ever existed in Burnett County." Camp Riverside and the boys who served there faded into the past. They built no monuments to themselves. All that remains are their stories. The trained eye can spot remains of the stone gate that once graced the entrance and the chimney of the officers quarters above the overgrown lilac bushes. Strolling the sidewalks one can find the ramp where the trucks were oiled, exposed bed springs in a cement foundation, steel support stakes of the water tower[180] and, behind the officers' quarters, the tombstone of Jesse Earl 1879-1959.

Section 21

Civilian Conservation Corps Roster

The following Civilian Conservation Corps rosters acknowledge those who were the work force behind the CCC accomplishments. Their individual efforts made the CCC the success that it was. Because actual lists of enrollees could not be found, rosters were created using a variety of resources. The following names were gleaned from local newspapers, CCC inspection reports, Riverside camp newspaper, CCC Alumni newsletters, Sparta District Annuals, autographs and oral history. Poor copy, use of nicknames, varied spellings and failing memory make it impossible to create a complete and accurate list. If you know of someone who is not included please notify the Burnett County Historical Society.

The index includes Riverside CCC Camp Roster, Minong Camp Roster, and a listing of boys from Burnett County who were in the CCC but not necessarily at Riverside Camp. It was often difficult to determine on which list a name belonged. A boy from Burnett County may have been in the CCC but the camp in which he served was not known. Some boys who served at Riverside Camp may have originated from somewhere else but remained in Burnett County following their discharge thus becoming part of the local community.

The Minong Camp Roster was included because in June of 1935 Riverside Camp split, one half of the enrollees transferring to Minong to form Camp 3661 S-106. Two years later in September of 1937, Camp Minong closed and the enrollees were transferred to Camp Riverside. Many of the enrollees at Camp Minong were enrollees at Camp Riverside either at the initiation of Camp Minong or at its closing.

If you had a family member in the CCC and would like to know more about their experience you may obtain their personnel records by writing the Personnel Records Center, Civilian Personnel Records, 111 Winnebago Street, St. Louis, M.O. 63118. Include as much information as possible with your request: name used in the CCC, Social Security Number, date and place of birth, federal employment agency which in this case is the CCC, dates when in the CCC, CCC camp in which employed, and if deceased proof of death.

The Power of Sand – Burnett County Civilian Conservation Corps

Riverside Camp summer of 1937.

Left page

First Row: Francis Quigley, Robert Kaminski, Matt Rautio, Kenneth Lundgren, Ray Anderson, Elmer Keppen, Arnold Block, Robert Jackelen, Irvine Melin, Bennie Tarbox.
Second Row: Dennis Cornelison, George Davis, William Sackett, Hobert Jansen, Harold Brewer, Hugh Blair, Woodrow Rabideau, Charles Tschumperlin, Byron Kain, Garth Ravey, Edwin Braaten, Kenneth Weeks, William Oranger, Kenneth Ball, Alfred Briggs.
Third Row: George Chase, Donald Moschel, Elmer Depner, Herbert Sewall, James Chapman, Edwin Wold, Alfred Millitte, Martin Frasl, Alex Kaszubowski, Roy Blandford, Walter Newcomb, Lester Gunem.
Fourth Row: Philip Coppens, Paul Vacho, Arthur Dishaw, Juluis Slonski, Merle Hanson, Ray Traczyk, Harold Goodman, Jay King, Lestern Johnson, Roy Taft, Alvin Zeffery, Louis Tomasowich.

Right page

First Row: Leonard Schultz, Lyle Frederick, Clarence Gruentzel, Ray Noel, Francis Faehling, Elmer Bruch, John Drew.
Second Row: Marvin Dishaw, Edwin Vobejda, Morgan Huglen, Ellery Hansen, Leonard Davy, Harold Jeffers, Stephan Maytan, Fred Kunkel, Kenneth Sweedey, Bernard Brault, John Johnson, John Mikolojak, Harris Larson.
Third Row: Harold Sigal, Pearl Jacobs, Malcolm Murphy, Steve Pagac, Ray Peterson, Bob Simons, Leonard Johnson, Gene Armstrong, Edward Freisleben, Roger Larson, John Frederick, Avery Wisner.
Fourth Row: Henry LeValley, Percy Spice, Douglas Fonstad, Robert Vincent, Leon Forsberg, Russell Knuth, Billy Jasicki, Donald Frank, Carroll Collier, Lloyd Wilson, Simon Barlow, Harold Harres.

Section 21 – Civilian Conservation Corps Roster

Portion of a 1935 or 1936 Riverside Camp photo.

71

The Power of Sand – Burnett County Civilian Conservation Corps

First row: 18. A.H. Stori, 19. O.B. Sykes, 20. J.F. Bukovsky, 21. Dennis Cornelison, 26. L.W. Johnson, 28. Garlen Ziehme,

Second row:
Third row: 38. Jaye King
Top row: 11. Lloyd Erickson, 13. Harvard Steingel.

Riverside Camp
August 4, 1938.

Section 21 – Civilian Conservation Corps Roster

Grantsburg Side Camp 1937

First Row: C. Lewandowski, Jesse Black, Arthur Schultz, Lyle Chelmo, Vernon Johnson, Marlo Jensen, Charles Thornton. Second Row: W. Gillis, Ronald Palmer, Rudolph Rolko, W. Szablewski, Martin Torgerson, Max Schilling, Frank Kollman.

Riverside Camp Roster

Army Personnel

Commanding Officers
Captain A. K. Stebbin - 1933
Captain Shutte - 1933-34
Captain J. P. Jensen - 1934
Lt. Trueman - 1935
Captain O. M. Jonas - 1935
Lt. Sture Ansel - 1935-36
Lt. Thomas W. DeMint - 1936
Captain P. L. Thompson - 1937
Captain O. B. Sykes - 1937-39
Lt. Edward E. Havlik - 1939
Lt. Edwin C. Ploetz - 1940
Captain Cochank - 1941
Lt. H. O. Neil - 1942
Lt. Wm. L. Prillmayer - 1942

Surgeon
Lt. Carl F. Waters M.D. - 1933-35
Lt. C. A. Faber - 1936
Lt. A. A. Svordin - 1936
Benjamin Kaplan M. D. - 1937
Lt. Carl F. Waters M. D. - 1938-40

Junior Officers
Lt. Geo J. Fieder
Lt. Sture Ansel
Lt. Ralph E. Lingren
Lt. Bieritz
Lt. C. W. Carson
Lt. J. F. Bukovsky
Lt. J. Mueller
Lt. J. M. Sturman
Lt. Clarence W. Huffman
Lt. Edwin C. H. Ploetz
A.G. Gullikson
Lt. Nelson

Educational Advisor
Harold H. Edwardson - 1934-36
Willard E. Osterhold - 1936
William L. Hadrich - 1937
A. H. Stori - 1938-39
Felix M. Shipp - 1939-40
Price George - 1940

Forestry Personnel

Superintendent
H. T. J. Cramer - 1933
Martin Johnston - 1934
M. M. DeBow 1934-1942

Forestry Personnel
Albert Hanson
Robert D. Baker
John Waggoner
Charles Maley
Wayne Wilcox
Claremont B. Miller
Keith Stafford
Mike J. O'Connell
Roy Guest
J. H. Crombie
Julius Radditz
Justin A. McCarthy
Martin C. Johnston
H. J. Kundert
Frank Maley
William O'Gara
John Heibel
Wilfred. H. Erickson
Alfred West
Norman C. Dunn
Henry Snyder
Donald Seeback
Carl J. Kielcheski
Philip G. Larson
Allan McVey
DeVere E. Button
DeLacy E Leichtnam
Russell G. Bartlein
Leo F. Cram
George E. Cutler

Riverside CCC Camp Enrollees

Stanley Abramson
Albin Adalphson
Adamizyk
Albert Aiello
Paul Akers
John Alkovich
Arthur D. Allickson
L. Allier
John Almquist
Alton Anderson
Floyd Anderson
Lester Anderson
Ray Anderson
Russell Anderson
Antonacci
Billy Armstrong
Gene Armstrong
Roy Armstrong
Carl Arthur
William Atkinson
Otto Aubert
David C. Bailey
Byron Baker
Kenneth Ball
Raymond W. Ballman
Bangora
Chauncey Bangs
Raymond Barber
Simon Barlow
Barnowski
Floyd Barret
Fay Barton
Eugene Barz
Bob Baustian
Lawrence Bavle
Justin Beebe
Beiderman
Belk

Harold Bell
F. Bellows
Leroy Bellows
Thomas Benge
Pete Benit
Benkowski
Fred Bergelson
Bergin
Gerald Berning
John Bertolino
Ludwig Bertram
Frank I. Bialozynski Jr.
Chet Biddle
Jesse Black
Hugh Blair
Roy Blandford
Van Blaricon
Arnold Block
Ernest A. Block
W. Blomquist
Morris E. Blosmore
Robert A. BoCaire
Bogdonas
Boguta
Theodore Bohenek
LeRoy J. Boll
Bollweg
George Bomband
William V. Borden
George W. Borg Jr
Felix Borio
Chuck Borner
Richard W. Bourn
Gregg F. Boyer
Edwin Braaten
Harold Brackeen
Bernard Brault
Paul Brehm

Harold Brewer
Kenneth Brewer
Alfred Briggs
William Broeffle
John Bronk
Zenith Browker
Dave Brown
Gilbert Brown
Jim Brown
Ray Brown
Robert Brown
William Brown
Walter Bruce
Elmer Bruch
Earl Bruhn
Nickolas G. Bugler
Alex Bumbar
Burns
Raymond S. Burzynski
Alfred Buskirk
Butler
Ralph E. Butts
Glen E. Cairns
Chester Cambell
Waldo Campes
Art Carlisle
A. Carlson
Harold Carter
Casey
John Cassin
Sam Catatonello
Jerome J. Ceel
Donald Cellebte
Frank Chapman
James Chapman
George Chase
Joe Chase
Lyle Chemo

74

Section 21 – Civilian Conservation Corps Roster

Arthur B. Cheney
Marvin Chipman
Christensen
Joe Cilib
Cilibrasi
Stewart Clark
Tom Clark
Steve Clementi
Joe Clemmer
Melin N. Clickner
Robert M. Cohen
Woodrow Colbert
James T. Colbeth
Milton S. Cole
Carroll Collier
Herbert H. Comdohr
Commdahi
Patrick Connolly
Ben Connors
Conoodaks
George Cooper
Lloyd Coos
Philip Coppens
Sabastain Corbino
Dennis Cornelison
Irish Coughlin
Jake Crandall
Tony J. Crivello
Leo Csoprigi
Henry Curd
Romaine Cyrus
Mitchel Czapka
Pike Dahlins
Dalke
Mike Daly
Francis G. Daniels
Norman Danielson
Daugherty
William Davey
George Davis
Lawrence Davis
Leonard Davy
Harold Day
Ralph V. Day
Ralph DeCapua
DeFrank
DeGrasse
Donald DeGreve
Harry DeLand
M. Delmonico
Kenneth W. DeLony
DeMacino
Walter Dempsey
Paul DeNicola
Bill Denniger
HPH Denniger
James Densmore
Elmer Depner
DeSimone
Raymond DesJardin
Joe Detratto

James Deverauox
James DeVito
Ralph DiCapua
Fernando B. Diez
Arthur Dishaw
Marvin Dishaw
Dolke
Emil Dolko
Domico
John Donaghue
Irvin E. Douville
Ralph Downs
John Drew
Vernon Driscoll
Drizzel
Drog
Dutch Drought
Everett A. Drought
Casey Duda
Jack D. Dugan
Dul
Ray Dunbar
John F. Dunn
Van Dusen
Edmund F. Dutkiewicz
Mike Dyda
Tony Dziuro
Jennie Earls
Harry Eber
Warren Edwards
Edwardson
Lee Eilmess
Steve Ekes
Alfred Eliason
Ernest C. Elliott
Elvin
Floyd Engebretson
M.L. Engebretson
Walter F. Engel
Al Engelhart
Duane D. Enger
Raymond England
Erwin W. Equitz Jr
Fred Erickson
Lloyd Erickson
Pete Erickson
Charles Eroncig
Mike Esposito
Evans
Harold Ewirs
Eyfield
Francis Fachling
Fredrick G. Fairbanks
Farickie
Farino
Freddie Felbab
Vernon Felio
Ferguson
Walter Ferret
John Festa
Fleskie

Harry Flick
Allen Flott
Flugstad
Fredie Folbab
Douglas Fonstad
Harry T. Forecki
Leon Forsberg
Irwin S. Fosmo
Francisco
Donald Frank
Jilek Frank
Raymond L. Frank
Martin Frasl
John Frederick
Lyle Frederick
Eugene A. Freeland
Kenneth P. Freiburger
Edward Freisleben
Carles H. Fristed
Leo N. Fristed
Charles A Fritschler
Frederick B. Fults
Merle Furman
Gabrielli
Andrew Galicki
Doc Gallagher
Henry J Gamer
John Gardner
Ike Garrett
Robert Gatten
Anthony J. Gebbia
Arthur Gerber
Gerlick
Gieger
Joe Gifford
Marvin Gilbertson
Albert C. Gill
William Gillis
Gobler
Goded
Peter Golden
Walter D. Gomulak
Elmer R. Goodenough
Harold Goodman
Alice Goon
Milton C. Gordon
Sid Gordon
Thomas Gordon
Gorman
Boob Gosar
Truman Gouchnaur
Chester Gradecki
Allen Gragen
Walter Grant
Roy Green
Greendeer
Stanley Gremban
Robert Gritzmacher
Harry Gross
Warren Grossman
J. Grubasta

Clarence Gruentzel
Vane Grushes
Alfred J. Guldvick
Lester Gunem
Gunum
Gust
Guy
Sylverter T. Guzinski
Fred Haaf
Harold W. Haaf
Blufford Hafford
Hahn
J. Halfield
Clifford Halvorson
Tomas Hamilton
Robert Hannus
Ellery Hansen
Bror E. Hanson
Herman A. Hanson
Merle Hanson
Harloy
Harold Harres
Leonard Hasse
Hastings
Jim Hatfield
Clifford Hattendorf
Clarence Hayden
Harold W. Hayden
Clarence Hedlund
Earl Heier
Orrin M. Helgeson
Delmer L. Henderson
Charles Henry
Ernest C. Hensey
George Herion
Franklin E. Herring
Chuck Herzberg
James Hester
Harold Hieles
Joseph Higgins
Arthur Hill
Ralph Hill
Herman Hines
Thomas Hinxch
A. Hinze
Haold E. Hix
Nicholas Hjdinovich
Norris Hoag
Vincent Hoey
Charles Hoffman
Hoic
Wilhelm Holden
M. Holmberg
Frank Holms
Melbourne Homberge
Hone
Melvin Hook
Ralph R. Hoover
Harry Hornke
Marshall Hotchkiss
Mike Hotchkiss

75

The Power of Sand – Burnett County Civilian Conservation Corps

Riverside Camp summer of 1939. First Row: K. Delong, W. Kistner, R. Bourn, M. Cole, N. Hjdinovich, C. Tschumperlin, W. LoJoie, R. Nordquist, N. Pagenkopf, O. Helgeson, J. Ivanis.
Second Row: E. Drought, J. Bronk, W. Bugler, E. Whiting, W. Borden, E. Muszynski, R. Johnston, D. Johson, F. Fairbanks, A. Kolodzyk, E. Equitz, A. Hoyt, E. Dutkiewicz, A. Guldvick, A. Gill, J.Dugan, W. Engel.
Third Row: L. Millette, L. Smith, J. Ceel, H. Johnson, G. Zinda, W. Rittenhouse, R. Springer, E. Michelbook, J. Ormston, S. Guzinski, L. Klimann, L. Wagner, L.H. Smith, S. Ekes, I. Douville.
Fourth Row: M. Clickner, J. Sieban, R. Ballman, H. Gamer, E. Studtman, L. Bavle, M. Blosmore, D. Stener, J. Peterson, F. Diez, G. Boyer, P. Moser, R. Barber, G. Schlief, J. Wallin, F. Fults.

Arnold L. Hoyt	Carl B. Johnson	Larry Kelly	Frank O. Kronberg
Arthur L. Hoyt	Carl V. Johnson	Roy Kelly	Joe Kruk
Hubert	Clarence Johnson	Alden R. Kelm	Roger Kulbeck
Ashley A. Hughes	Donald M. Johnson	Pat Kenway	Alfred Kuldvick
George Hugie	Earl Johnson	Earl K. Keppen	Fred H. Kunkel
Morgan Huglen	Harry J. Johnson	Elmer Keppen	Erving Labecki
Clifford Hunt	Hollis Johnson	Joe Kewitz	LaBonte
Clyde Hunt	John Johnson	J. Kigahns	Walter L. LaJoie
Ralph Hunter	Leonard W. Johnson	Carleton King	L'Allier
William L. Hunter	Lestern Johnson	Jay King	Alvin Lammert
Illkanich	Martin Y. Johnson	Rex Kirkwood	Clarence Lang
Archie Isaacson	Roy Peter Johnson	Wendell J. Kistner	Claude Larrabee
Joseph Ivanis	S.M.R. Johnson	Fay Kitchel	Earl Larrabee
Harold Ivers	S. R. H. Johnson	LaVerne Klemann	Buster Larson
Robert Jackelen	Vernon Johnson	Johnny Klodinskie	Harris Larson
Victor Jackson	Robert Johnston	Klodzly	Ivan H. Larson
Pearl M. Jacobs	George Jolley	Bruno Kmiec	Leslie Larson
Pee W. Jacobs	Jones	Russell Knuth	Nathan Larson
Jacobson	Jorgenson	Morgan O. Knutson	Roger Larson
Clifford Jahnsen	Jurrisisin	Irwin Koenig	Bill Laue
Frank Jajko	Michael Jurscism	Kokumo	Hank LaValley
Stanley Jankowki	George Kachala	William Kolbrek	Sherman S. Lawler
Hobert Jansen	Bruno Kaice	Charles Kollman	Lawson
Peter Janusak	Byron Kain	Frank Kollman	Lazanski
Anthony Januska	Robert Kaminski	Arthur L. Kolodzyk	Thomas M. Lee
Roy Jarvis	Harry Kampka	John Koloski	Lester J. Leef
Billy Jasicki	Myles Kasmiersyk	Anthony Kolter	Maxwell Leggett
Harold Jeffers	Adam Kasprosak	Frank Koman	Alton Lein
Jennings	Tony Kasprozak	Kozenski	Wilfred LeMay
Marlo Jensen	Alex Kaszubowski	Kranz	William LeMere
Johnny	Steve Katon	Charles E. Krebs	Lenoc
Lawrence Johnsen	Ted Kazmerski	Tyler Krieps	Edward Lepinski
Bill Johnson	Jim Kearney	Lawrence A. Kringle	Levison

76

Section 21 – Civilian Conservation Corps Roster

First Row: A. Olson, H. Forecki, S. Lawler, F. Jacobs, E. Block, W. Hunter, F. Herring, R. Roehl, G. Hugle, L. Tucker, L. Johnson, G. Patnode.
Second Row: G. Cairns, C. Fristed, A. Myers, H. Hanson, R. Mortson, E. Nelson, G.L. Ziehme, C. Jahnsen, L.W. Johnson, A. Cheney, P. Jacobs, F. Bialoszynski, F.H.Kunkel, R. Buzynski, R. BoCaire, P. DeNicole, L. Snow, A. Lockwood, E. Myers.

Third Row: V. Felio, T. Lee, D. Bailey, A. Hughes, R. Frank, H. Stengel, J. Dunn, C. Fritschler, R. Rylander, F. Scott, L. Peak, W. Gomulak, L. Mingo, E. Elliot, D. Henderson, C. Segelstrom, M. Olaon, L. Fristed.
Fourth Row: J. Taylor, R. Peterson, C. Gradecki, H. Comdohr, P. Tischman, A. Allickson, D. Peterson, J. Scheufeli, M. Moser, R. Taft, A. Shielman, F. Pickham, A. Smith, D. Wedin, R. Hoover, E. Fosmo.

C. Lewandowski	John Maul	Ted Milowski	Thrase Nepperly
Ted Lewis	Edwin Carl Maxwell	Lawrence H. Mingo	G. Ness
Ervin Libecki	Mayer	Tony Mitas	Melvin Newcomb
Lieb	Stephan Maytan	Mitchel	Walter Newcomb
Russel E. Lien	McCardle	Lyle Mitelade	Murl Newhorter
Linders	Donald McCarthy	Frank Moll	Joe Newitz
Vernon Linquist	Justin McCarthy	Mollicco	Vernon Nienas
Floyd Linz	Leslie McCauly	Molly	Ray Noel
Lioce	McCumber	Bob Moore	Roy V. Nordquist
Livingston	Alex McDonald	Franklin M. Moritz	Red Norwood
Allyn H. Lockwood	Richard McFadden	Morris	Steve Novak
Lonke	Jim McFaddin	Frank Morrow	Harry Novoral
Lorrakkers	Michael McHugh	Robert C. Mortson	Shorty Nykanon
Oscar Lovinson	Albert McLain	Donald Moschel	Harlan L. Oberg
Henry Lowe	Red McLain	Martin P. Moser	Peter O'Herron
Frank Lucarz	Wilfred McNeal	Peter V. Moser	Howard J. Ohlson
Zigge Lugoski	Irvine Melin	Moskal	Olenik
Steve Lukis	Warren H. Melin	Moss	Arnold E. Olson
Bert Lund	Charles R. Melquist	Mueller	Clifford E. Olson
Kenneth Lundgren	DuWayne Mercer	Mullinix	Marvin K. Olson
George Machala	Jerome S. Meronek	John H. Munz	Bill Omelanchek
Malinowski	Murl B. Mewhorter	Malcolm Murphy	William Oranger
Mallek	Carroll F. Meyer	Murry	Forest Orbell
James Manning	Eddie Meyer	Edward J. Muszynski	Jack O. Ormston
Blaine B. Manor	Harold Meyers	Andrew Myers	Orr
Bob Manz	Everett A. Michelbook	Eugene A Myers	Leon Oslund
Orville J. Marks	John Mikolojak	Robert Nalipinski	Edward O'Toole
T. Marquis	C. Mikrut	Stanley Nary	Henry Ourd
C. Martin	Clairmonte B. Miller	Claude Nelson	Chester Paczkowski
Henry A. Martin	Doyle Miller	Eldon L. Nelson	Edward Padsiadly
Kelly Martin	Walter Miller	John Nelson	Steve Pagac
Francis Martineau	Alfred Millette	Maurice Nelson	Norman F. Pagenkopf
Claude Matthews	Louis T. Millette	Neness	A. Palmer

The Power of Sand – Burnett County Civilian Conservation Corps

Riverside Camp summer of 1940.
First row: 27. Douglas Wedin.
Second row: 6. Sebatian, 12. Briggs, 14. Warren Melin, 18. Pete Erickson, 20. Lt. Ploetz, 22. Al C. Zinda, 30. Dennis Peterson
Third row: 4. Norris Hoag, 7. Paul Akers, 9. Erwin Fosmo
Top row: 7. Ivol Paulus, 17. Art Allickson, 19. Nathan Larson, 25. Garlen Ziehme, 29. Smith, 34. Harlan Oberg.

Ronald Palmer	Jack Putness	Leslie A. Rosenberg	Bud Schreiber
Joe Paluga	Quedo	Alex Rosio	Everett Schroeder
Arthur Pankiewicz	Francis Quigley	Joseph Ross	Alfred Schultz
Amiel Panser	Woodrow Rabideau	Rudty	Arthur Schultz
Maniel Panser	Jules Radditz	Warner Rueline	Leonard Schultz
Gerald K. Patnode	Arnold Ranta	Leo Rueter	Ben Schuster
Paulserude	Paul Rasmussen	Art Ruicker	Schwenn
Ival Paulus	W. Ratliff	Joe Rychtarick	William Scotka
Jim Pavlinec	Matt Rautio	Ted Ryczek	Floyd A. Scott
LeRoy E. Peak	Garth Ravey	Stanley Ryeczyk	Harold R. Scott
Wilmer Pearson	Recke	Glen Rylander	Sebastian
Floyd E. Peckham	J. Reddsville	Richard L. Rylander	Clarence Segelstrom
Perkins	Ray Reily	Ted Rylander	Selmyht
Hubert Persons	Mike Rennis	Ryscek	Lawrence Severson
John Peters	Leslie H. Rhode	Edward Saak	Herbert Sewell
Alden Peterson	Virgil A. Rhode	William Sackett	John Seyka
Dennis Peterson	Dusty Rhodes	Leonard St. John	Pat Shelton
Fred Peterson	Harold Rhodes	Sajec	Norman Shewmake
Harlod D. Peterson	Ries	Walter Samsel	Donald Shogren
Johnnie M. Peterson	Glen A Rigsby	Duan Sandberg	Roy Short
Ray Peterson	Paul Rimus	Sanborn	George Shriver
Richard Peterson	Ripey	Arnold Sander	Wayne Shumate
Robert T. Peterson	Wendal Ristner	Harry Sanders	John Sieben
Harold M. Phernetton	William C. Rittenhouse	George Santos	Harold Sigal
Manley Phersdorf	Edward Roach	Sasse	Andrew Simms
Thomas Philbin	Marvin E. Roatch	Robert Schaefer	Lee Simms
Stanley Pikula	Paul Roberts	Bill Schaff	Bob Simons
Plaski	Roebarge	Art Scheney	Skaife
Henry Poeschl	Gus Roebke	John Scheufeli	Frank P. Skiba
Potter	Robert P. Roehl	Max Schilling	Skudlarzk
Powell	Buster Rojer	Galen L. Schlief	Slominski
Gerald Pratt	Rudolph Rolko	George Schmidt	Juluis Slonski
Lyle Price	Rombalski	Jerome Schneider	Lyle Smedegard

Section 21 – Civilian Conservation Corps Roster

Alfred E. Smith	Ed Stumo	Bernard Trudeau	Lloyd Wilson
Dick Smith	Kenneth Sturgeon	Charles C. Tschumperlin	Woodrow Wilson
Earl Smith	Sufficool	Lyle F. Tucker	Jack Winger
Lawrence E. Smith	Ivan Swanson	Tulip	Winton
Leonard H. Smith	Stanley Swanson	Turk	Vernon G. Wischer
Ronald E. Smith	Kenneth Swanstrom	Turner	Avery Wisner
Willis Smith	John D. Sweat	George Ulbricht	Wilfred Wisner
Leslie M. Snow	Kenneth Sweedey	Paul Vacho	Wjott
James Somzela	Swensen	VanDusen	Edwin Wold
Alfred Sonetay	Henry Swiderski	Rudy Vezmar	Herman Wold
Edwin C. Songetay	W. Szablewski	Robert Vincent	Steve Wuzaszewski
Percy Spice	Szablinski	Jack Vineyard	Anton Wyzgowski
E. Spieler	Tackett	Edwin Vobejda	H. Yaugha
Arnold H. Spielman	Marvin A. Taeuber	Steve Waclowski	Farmer Young
Robert M. Springer	Henry Taft	John C. Waggoner	Charley Yushkovich
R. Stack	Roy A. Taft	Ludwig F. Wagner	Edward Zaba
Kenny Stafford	Stanley Tamolunis	Waldvogel	Stanley Zajac
Kid Stahl	Bennie Tarbox	John D. Wallin	Oliver Zank
Elie Stanich	Harley Taylor	Ziggie Walzyk	Zatko
Stasho	Joseph E. Taylor	Douglas E. Wedin	Alvin Zeffery
Russell Stein	Francis Tharaldson	Kenneth Weeks	Joseph Zemkus
Harvard Steingle	Charles Thornton	Welch	Garlen Ziehme
David B. Stener	Thors	Grenfall Wells	Al C. Zinda
Peter Stepulin	Merle Thurman	LeRoy Wells	Gerald G. Zinda
Stevenson	Thurstin	Milton J. Westrom	Zrinpano
Clark Stewart	Phillip A. Tischman	Ed Werdier	Zurawski
Russell Stewart	Louis Tomasowich	Raymond Westland	
Elmer Stoddard	Joe Tomaszewski	Paul Westring	
Joseph Stopulin	Tomczak	Philip Wieble	
Jessie E. Stover	Bill Tongue	Wiedling	
Frederic Strautt	Martin Torgerson	Laverne E. Williams	
Edmund H. Studtman	Ray Traczyk	Otis Williams	
Clarence Stulen	Gene Trichie	Monk Wilmont	

79

Minong Camp Roster
Army Personnel

Commanding Officers
Capt. Jonas
Capt. Orin B. Sykes

Junior Officers
Lt. Sturman
Lt. P. P. Meshkoff
Lt. Bieritz
Lt. George W. Pinnell

Surgeon
Lt. Richard Matthies
Lt. Carl F. Waters

Educational Advisor
Arnold H. Stori

Project Superintendent
Duncan Cameron

Project Foreman
Floyd Gobler
Roy Guest
Eldon Marple
Roy Goodwill
Andrew A. Fisk
Solon A. Bott
Dan Leach
H. R. Blevin
Leo F. Cram
Thane Brown
Norman C. Dunn

Minong CCC Camp Enrollees

Wanta Ambrose
H. Bailey
W. Baranowski
Otto W. Bay
Vincent J. Belisle
Owen L. Bender
M. Bengtson
V. Bengtson
Louis F. Benkowski
Willis E. Books
George S. Bores
S. Bortas
James H. Bortha
E. Bowen
Irving S. Brandt
Lawrence J. Brouillette
George E. Brown
Ernest T. Butkovich
John Cadman
William O. Carley
Alfred J. Christie
A. B. Crane
George G. Dawa
John W. Dosch
Arthur K. Drake
Elvin R. Ellefson
Robert L. Engel
W. Exner
Raymond N. Gargaro
C. Gavin
Peter P. Gavinski
Albert A. Gehrman
Edgar L. Gehrman

Elmer D. Gerlach
J. Hajek
C. Heinisch
Carl E. Helm
H. Hill
L. Hiller
Mike Hohenzy
Earl Holst
Boyd Hoover
Henry R. Jacobs
L. Jarchow
Joseph Jaros
C. Jayroe
DeWayne Jenson
Louis I Jesse
Paul R. Jevne
Russell E. Johnston
Peter Jozwiak
Edwin V. Jurgella
Raymond R. Jurgella
Alex J. Kaszubski
George G. Kawa
James Kearney
Ronald K. King
R. Koelbl
Francis C. Kondzella
Chester Kowalski
Robert A. Krasavage
Charles R. Krebs
Okley J. Kummer
Roman N. Kurzinski
Ivan H. Larson
Lester L. Larson

DeLacy E. Leichtnam
Allyn H. Lockwood
Eugene H. Locy
Herbert G. Lom
Fred E. Manning
Robert D. Martin
Manville Martinson
A. Mattson
George R. Mayne
John S. Micklin
Lawrence C. Miller
Theodore H. Muenster
Ira D. Nelson
R. Nelson
A. New
Frank Norwid
Louis L. Nuenke
Marvin L. Nyman
Arnold E. Olson
Clifford E. Olson
Rueben G. Olson
P. Pagel
W. J. Pankratz
Earl Parizo
L. Peterson
Marshal E. Peterson
John W. Potter
Paul R. Prim
Frank L. Ray
Leonard Repinski
Albert M. Repka
Julius E. Richards
John J. Roman

Glen F. Rylander
C. Schenk
Theodore J. Schubert
Robert A Schultz
Clarence G. Schwebke
Rudolph A. Secky
Edward Sherley
Lowell G. Shoquist
Wayne A. Shumate
L. J. Sierzchulski
Gerald E. Simonis
Lyle B. Smedegard
Ronald E. Smith
M. Stajniger
Stanley F. Stockfish
Roy Strand
M. Thomas
John P. Thornton
Lewis E. Titel
Frank Topol
Harold H. Turner
Joe N. Volovsek
Albin J. Wanta
Donald G. Winchell
Edmund H. Worzalla
Alvin J. Yeager
C. Yushkevich
Ernest J. Zaborowski
Adam F. Zakrzewski
Joseph J. Zemkus
Garlen Ziehme
Sylvester S. Zoop

Section 21 – Civilian Conservation Corps Roster

CCC Enrollees from Burnett County

Stanley Adams
Ralph Allier
Alfton Anderson
David Anderson
John Anderson
Oliver Anderson
Ryland Anderson
Virgil Anderson
John Andresen
Russell Atkinson
Otto Aubert
Stanley Augustine
Eugene Bailey
Albert Baker
Byron Baker
Raymond Barber
Bob Baustian
Albert Bearhart
Russell Bentley
Max Biederman
Arnold Block
Donald Brager
Merle Brekke
Alfred Briggs
James Briggs
Ralph Briggs
Billy Broeffle
Lloyd Brown
William Brown
Dr. Budd's son
Alfred Buskirk
Elmer Buskirk
Glen Cairns
Ellsworth Carlson
John E. Carlson
Walter Carlson
Ernest Carpenter
Lyle Chelmo
Merle Chelmo
Arthur Cheney
Ken Christianson
Vernon Christner
Perry Clapsaddle
Junior Clark
Paul Cook
Lloyd Coos
Melvin Corner
Lyle Cyrus
Myron Dahl
Norman Danielson
Clarence Davis
Leon Davis
Richard Davis
Ernest Denotter
J. Robert Dietrich
Louie Doetsch
Albert DuBois
Jay Dufty
John Dunn

Warren Edwards
Conrad Eklof
Alfred Eliason
Raymond Ellis
Floyd Engebretson
M. L. Engebretson
Alfred Engelhart
Raymond England
Alvin Erickson
Lloyd Erickson
Wally Falgstad
Irwin Fosmo
Glen Fossum
Raymond Franzeen
Everett Fremont
Carles Fristed
Leo Fristed
Walter Fristed
James Frizzell
Lavern Gabert
Dennis Gatten
Edwin Gatten
Preston Gatten
Robert Gatten
Al Gere
Albert Gill
John V. Gomulak
Harry Goodell
Morton Goodell
Harold Goodman
David Graf
Francis Grant
Walter Grant
Robert Gritzmacher
Vane Grushus

John Gumulak
William Guy
Alfred Haaf
Fred Haaf
Harold Haaf
Lorain Halberg
Clifford Halvorson
Robert Halvorson
Wilfred Hamilton
Art Hammer
Albert Hanson
George E. Hanson
Otto Hanson
John Hartshorn
Raymond Hartshorn
Clarence Hayden
Red Hayden
Clarence Hedlund
Earl Heier
John Heier
Frank Heilig
Delmer Henderson
Joe Herzog
Alvin Higgins
Ralph Hill
Barney Hills
Chester Hills
Harold Hills
Howard Hills
Herman Hinz
John Hinz
Howard Hitchcock
Norris Hoag
Albert Holmberg
Axel Holmes

Mike Hotchkiss
Harold Hoyt
Ralph Hunter
Richard Hunter
Virgil Hutten
Donald Jensen
Lewis Jensen
Marlo Jensen
Rueben Jensen
Fred Jiles
John Jiles
Archie Johnson
Carl B. Johnson
Earl Johnson
Edwin Johnson
Herman Johnson
Hollis Johnson
Lawrence Johnson
Leonard Johnson
Leroy Johnson
Leslie Johnson
Vernon Johnson
Robert Kaminski
Earl Keppen
Elmer Keppen
Fay Ketchel
Al Keyes
Carleton King
LaVerne Klemann
Lawrence Kringle
Henry Kubicka
Paul Kuhnley
Albert Kulbeck
Roger Kulbeck
Fritz Kunkel

Grantsburg Ranger Station, Grantsburg, Wisconsin.

81

Howard Lang
Claude Larrabee
Earl Larrabee
Arnold Larson
Gunnard Larson
Ivan Larson
Leslie Larson
Lewis Larson
Myron Larson
Nathan Larson
Russell Larson
Walter Larson
Lester Leef
Hector Lien
Russell Lien
Arnold Lindberg
Kenneth Love
Bert Lund
Vernon Lundquist
Harold Malone
Joe Marcoon
Sis Markus
Henry Martin
Howard McCann
James McCann
James McCarthy
Nebal McCarthy
Merritt McDowell
Cleon McFaggen
Lyle McKee
Wilfred McNeal
Irvine Melin
Warren Melin
Charles Melquist
Jerome S. Meronek
Murl Mewhorter
Carol Meyer
Donald Miller
Thomas Miller
Walter Miller
George Millette
Lawrence H. Mingo
Frank Morrow
Milo Owen Morrow
Martin Moser
Robert Moulton
Martin Murphy
Claude Nelson
Harold Nelson
John Nelson
Melvin Newcomb
Richard Nordquist
Roy Nordquist
Leslie Norine
Henry Odden
Axel Olson
Jack Ormston
Leonard Ortendahl
Leon Oslund
Joseph Pagel
Roland Palm

David Papier
Milton Paul
Bob Paulus
Ival Paulus
Floyd Peckham
Harold A. Pederson
Arthur Peterson
Bud Peterson
Richard Peterson
Harold Phernetton
John Prichard
George Revor
William Revor
Rasmusson
Claude Richmond
William Rivard
Warner Rueline
Edwin Rylander
Glen Rylander
Lawrence Rylander
Duane Sandberg
Art Scheney
John Scheufeli
Francis Schmidt

Alvin Schultz
Chuck Scotka
Frank Scotka
William Scotka
Doug Sears
Clarence Segelstrom
Herbert Sewell
Donald Shogren
Ted Shoquist
John Sieben
John Smiley
Alfred Smith
Dick Smith
Earl Smith
Leslie Snow
Alfred Sonetay
Edwin Sonetay
George Springer
Harvey Springer
Robert Springer
Kenneth Stafford
George Staples
Harvard Steingle
Russell Stewart

Carl Lyle Stone
Frederic Strautt
Gunnard Swanson
Stanley Swanson
Kenneth Swanstrom
Ernie Tietz
Clarence Trumble
Henry VanLoo
Luke Waggoner
Ralph Wandby
Ed Werdier
Harold West
Ford Wester
Raymond Westland
Milton Westrom
Elmer Wicklund
Roy Wicklund
Conrad Wilson
William Wilson
Herman Wold
Vern Samuel Woods
Elmer Zach

Works Consulted

American Forests: The Magazine of the American Forestry Association, Washington D.C. July 1933. Quoted at "Civilian Conservation Corps." http://newdeal.feri.org/forests/af733.htm.

Athearn, Robert G. *The Roosevelt Era*. Vol. 14 of *The American Heritage*. New York, Dell Publishing Co. Inc.,1963.

Bardon MD, Richard and Nute, Grace Lee. *A Winter in the ST. Croix Valley George Nelson's Reminiscences 1802-1803*. Minnesota Historical Society, 1948.

Burmeister, Wayne. Interview with Maurice Heyer 2000.

Burmeister, Wayne. Interview with Roy Jarvis, 2000.

Burnett County Agriculture Statistical Series. Wisconsin Crop and Livestock Reporting Service, Madison, 1954.

Burnett County Almanac Living the Good Life 2003. Spooner, Wisconsin: Spooner Advocate.

Burnett County Enterprise. Webster Wisconsin.

Burnett County Forest History. Burnett County Forestry Office.

Burnett County Forest Tour, Second Annual, September 20, 1937, Program.

Burnett County Resorter. Grantsburg, Wisconsin: Journal Publishing Company, 1954.

Burnett County Schools, Listing of Graduates 1914-1960. Burnett County Historical Society.

Burnett County Sentinel. Grantsburg, Wisconsin.

Burnett County Siren. Siren, Wisconsin.

Carruth, Gorton. *What Happened When*. New York: Harper Collins Publishers Inc., 1989.

"Civilian Conservation Corps." http://www.cccalumni.org/states/wisconsin1.html

"Roosevelt's Tree Army." http://www.cccalumni.org/history1.html

Civilian Conservation Corps, Pictorial Review Sparta District 1939. Burnett County Historical Society.

Civilian Conservation Corps Program Reports, 1933-1942. Box 1 & 10 National Archives and Records Administration, Great Lakes Region, Chicago, Illinois.

Civilian Conservation Corps, Riverside Camp Map. Burnett County Historical Society.

Civilian Conservation Corps, Riverside Camp Lake Improvement Maps for Devils and Yellow Lakes. Burnett County Historical Society.

Civilian Conservation Corps, Riverside Tree Planting and Survival Assessment Maps. Burnett County Historical Society.

Civilian Conservation Corps, Sparta District Annual 1937. Burnett County Historical Society.

Cohen, Stan. *The Tree Army, A Pictorial History of the Civilian Conservation Corps, 1933-1942*. Missoula, Montana: Pictorial Histories Publishing Company, 1980.

Conkin, Paul K. *The New Deal*. Arlington Heights, Illinois: Harlan Davidson, Inc., 1975.

Conservation Commission Records Series 271, Box 899-900, Wisconsin State Historical Society.

Crex Meadows Wildlife Area Self-Guided Auto Tour. Wisconsin Department of Natural Resources Grantsburg, Wisconsin.

Crex Meadows Wildlife Area. Wisconsin Department of Natural Resources, Grantsburg, Wisconsin.

Danbury Fire Investigation Report, June 19, 1939.

Death Certificates for Stanley Tamulonis and George Conrad Ulbricht. Burnett County Register of Deeds.

E. C. W. 53-S WORK PROJECTS. August 1, 1935. Burnett County Historical Society.

Events That Shaped the Century of *Our American Century*. Alexandria, Virginia: Time-life Books, 1998.

Evert Family Papers 1880-1943. Wisconsin State Historical Society.

Evert, Fred. *Burnett County: A Handbook for Veterans and Home Seekers*. Burnett County, Wisconsin, 1946. Burnett County Historical Society.

Funk & Wagnalls New Encyclopedia. New York: Funk & Wagnalls Inc., 1979.

Fure, Carole. Interview with Byron Baker 2003.

Fure, Carole. Interview with Myron Dahl 2003.

Fure, Carole. Interview with John Dunn 2003.

Fure, Carole. Interview with Maurice Heyer 2003.

Fure, Carole. Interview with Norris Hoag 2003.

Fure, Carole. Interview with Bert Lund 2003.

Fure, Carole. Interview with Warren Melin 2004.

Fure, Carole. Interview with Roy Nordquist 2003.

Fure, Carole. Interview with Beatrice Olson 2003.

Fure, Carole. Interview with Ivol Paulus 2003.

Fure, Carole. Interview with Mrs. Helen Quigley, 2003.

Fure, Carole. Interview with Duane Sandberg 2003.

Fure, Carole. Interview with Charles Scotka 2003.

Fure, Carole. Interview with Harvard Stengal 2000.

Fure, Carole. Interview with Russell Stewart 2003.

Fure, Carole. Interview with Phil Stromberg 2003.

Glad, Paul W. *The History of Wisconsin Vol. V. War, a New Era and Depression 1914-1940.* Stevens Point, Wisconsin: Worzalla Publishing Company, 1990.

Hinckley Fire. Askov, Minnesota: American Publishing Company, 1976.

Inter-County Leader. Frederic, Wisconsin.

Journal of Burnett County. Grantsburg, Wisconsin.

Koselak, Janine and Hill, Linda. *National Public Lands Day Celebrates the Civilian Conservation Corps.* BLM National Science and Technology Center, 2001.

Land Record Vol. 200 page 529. Burnett County Register of Deeds.

Leader. Fredcric, Wisconsin.

Leopold, Aldo. *A Sand County Almanac*. New York: Oxford University Press, 1969.

Lewis, Lydia Longwell. "CCC: $1-a-day, Work Welcomed." *Spooner Advocate* November 1983-84.

"Natural Resources of Wisconsin." *Wisconsin Blue Book 1964*. Burnett County Historical Society.

Official Proceedings of Burnett County Board of Supervisors, 1921, 1932, 1937. Burnett County Historical Society.

Olson, Dave and Bickford, Norm. Burnett County Forestry History notes, 1986. Burnett County Historical Society.

Ostergren, Robert C. and Vale, Thomas R. *Wisconsin Land and Life*. Madison: University of Wisconsin Press, 1997.

Peet, Ed L. *Burnett County Wisconsin*. The Journal of Burnett County, Grantsburg, Wisconsin, 1902. Burnett County Historical Society.

Quigley, John. Personnel Record 1934-1937. National Personnel Records Center, St. Lois, Missouri.

Rivers: Ribbons of Life. Burnett County Land & Water Conservation Department, 2000. Burnett County Historical Society.

Riverside CCC, Thanksgiving Dinner Menu.

Riverside Low Down. Riverside CCC Camp Newspaper 1935-1936. Burnett County Historical Society.

Salmond, John A. *The Civilian Conservation Corps, 1933-1942: A New Deal Case Study*. Durham, North Carolina: Duke University Press, 1976.

Semo, John V. *The Story of Camp Pattison*. Wisconsin Department of Natural Resources, PUB-PR-282 2003.

Superior Evening Telegram. Superior, Wisconsin.

The Spooner Ranger Station 1928-1986. Burnett County Historical Society.

Wisconsin Blue Book 1917. Burnett County Historical Society.

Wisconsin Blue Book 1905. Burnett County Historical Society.

Wisconsin Conservation Department. Timber Sale Report. Sale No. 1.

The Wisconsin Cartographers' Guild. *Wisconsin's Past and Present, A Historical Atlas*. Madison, Wisconsin, University of Wisconsin Press, 1998.

Wisconsin State Planning Board and Conservation Commission. *A Park, Parkway and Recreational Area Plan. Bulletin No. 8*. Madison, Wisconsin, January 1939. Burnett County Historical Society.

Endnotes

[1] *Crex Meadows Auto Tour* No. 14.
[2] *Burnett County Almanac 2003.*
[3] Ostergren p49. Natural Resources of Wisconsin, *Blue Book 1964,* p77-82. Wisconsin State Planning Board p101. Evert, *Burnett County Handbook* p2.
[4] Ostergren p49. Natural Resources of Wisconsin, *Blue Book 1964,* p77-82. Wisconsin State Planning Board p101. Evert, *Burnett County Handbook* p2.
[5] Natural Resources of Wisconsin, *Blue Book 1964* p78.
[6] *Crex Meadows Auto Tour* No. 13. Wisconsin State Planning Board p106-107. Fure Interview with Phil Stromberg.
[7] Burnett County Agriculture p6,9.
[8] Bardon p41.
[9] Peet p27, 46.
[10] Natural Resources of Wisconsin, Blue Book 1964. Glad p203-204.
[11] Natural Resources of Wisconsin, Blue Book p58.
[12] Ostergren p27-28.
[13] Glad p200-201, 207-208.
[14] Glad p208-209. Natural Resources of Wisconsin, Blue Book p56-60.
[15] "Accept Burnett Lands Under Forest Crop Law" *Journal* March 24, 1932. "Forestry Partnership" Journal February 22, 1934. "Committee Hears Burnett County Tax Problems" Journal September 24, 1931. "Burnett County Delinquency Is 93,000 Acres" Journal December 29, 1932. Glad p209. Ostergren p464. Natural Resources of Wisconsin, Blue Book p58. Burnett County Forest History.
[16] *The Spooner Ranger Station* p24.
[17] *The Spooner Ranger Station.* E.C.W. 53-S Work Projects Map.
[18] "Who Causes Forest Fires?" Journal May 15, 1932.
[19] Glad p209.
"Town Chairmen Voice Approval Of Land Zoning" *Journal* February 22, 1934. "Zoning Meetings In Burnett County" *Journal* September 13, 1934. Burnett County Forest History. Evert, *Burnett County Handbook*, p2.
[20] "Local Settlers Among 400 to Benefit By Move To Better Land" *Journal* March 8, 1934. "May Relocate 14 Residents" *Journal* October 13, 1938. "County Has 76,338 Acres Land Under Forest Crop" *Journal* December 7, 1939. "Federal Government Buys Land in Burnett County" *Journal* November 30, 1936. Burnett County Forest History.
[21] "$88,500 Returned Delinquent On 1932 County Tax Roll" *Journal* July 13, 1933.
[22] "County Commissioners Reduce Salaries of Burnett Officials" *Journal* November 19, 1931. "Schools Receive Only 54 Per Cent of Aid Due From State" *Journal* December 21, 1933. "Reduce Wage of Village Teachers For Next Term" *Journal* April 7, 1932. "County Set-Up Organized for Relief of Poor" *Journal* August 25, 1932.
[23] "1932 The Great Depression" *Events That Shaped the Century.* p82. Athearn p1175-1181.
[24] "1932 The Great Depression" *Events That Shaped the Century,* p82.
[25] "1933 FDR's First 100 Days" *Events That Shaped the Century,* p86. Athearn p1181-1183. "Civilian Conservation Corps" *Funk & Wagnall* p157. "New Deal" Funk & Wagnall p277. "Roosevelt, Franklin Delano, The Presidency" *Funk & Wagnall* p387. Glad p493. Conkin p1-19. Koselak.
[26] Cohen p6, 176. "Forestry" *Funk & Wagnall* p185.
[27] Salmond "New Deal" *Funk & Wagnall* p277. "Roosevelt, Franklin Delano, The Presidency" *Funk & Wagnall* p387.
[28] Glad p495-496.
[29] Glad p497.
[30] Glad p493. *American Forests.*
[31] Glad p493. Athearn p1183.
[32] "County Quota Set at 30 For Forest Project" *Journal* May 4, 1933.
[33] Conversation with Marcus Nelson. "Company 626" *CCC Pictorial Review.*
[34] *Riverside Low Down* July 26, 1935.
[35] *The Spooner Ranger Station* p35.
[36] "Danbury" *Journal* August 10, 1933.
[37] "Dennis Gatten Writes From CC Camp At Westboro" *Journal* November 30, 1933.
[38] *Riverside Low Down* May 24, 1935.
[39] Inspection Report February 23, 1934, CCC Program Reports.

[40] *Riverside Low Down* November 20, 1936. Fure. Interview with Warren Melin
[41] *Riverside Low Down* November 22, 1935, February 1936.
[42] Burmeister interview with Roy Jarvis, 2000.
[43] Salmond. *Riverside Low Down* July 26, 1935. Fure. Interview with Maurice Heyer 2003.
[44] Cohen p8,31. Salmond. CCC Enrollees, Local Experienced Men, April 15, 1937, Conservation Commission Records.
[45] Inspection Report June 11, 13, 1935, CCC Program Reports. Personnel Record of Millard M. DeBow, Conservation Commission Records.
[46] *Riverside Low Down* July 24, 1936.
[47] "CCC Boys Clear Land For Summer Residence Here" *Journal*. April 19, 1934. "Danbury" *Journal* May 3, 1934. *Riverside Low Down* April 24, 1936.
[48] *Riverside Low Down* July 24, August 14, 28, 1936.
[49] *Riverside Low Down* October 25, September 27, 1935, April 24, 1936. Work Plan for April 1937-June 1938, Conservation Commission Records. Intra-Office Memorandum October 17, 1935, Conservation Commission Records. "Largest Fire of This Season In West Marshland" *Journal* August 6, 1936. "Conduct County Water Survey For Forest Fire Suppression" *Journal* August 12, 1937. "Riverside CCC News" *Journal* June 29, 1939. "128 Residents Make Annual Tour" *Journal* September 23, 1937.
[50] *The Spooner Ranger Station* p1-35. E. C. W. 53-S Work Projects #51, 55, 80. "Phone Line Will Connect Fire Towers" *Journal* June 29, 1939. "Will Continue To Operate Civilian Riverside Camp" *Journal* October 7, 1937. "Company 626" *CCC Pictorial Review*. Work Plan 1937-1938. Conservation Commission Records. "Pick Wardens To Fight Fires" *Journal* March 30, 1939.
[51] "Conservation Workers To Be Fire Observers" *Journal* March 5, 1934. "Will Give Vets Preference In CCC Enrollment" *Journal* April 5, 1934. Inspection Reports November 15, 1934, June 8, 1935, CCC Program Reports. Work Plan 1937-1938. Conservation Commission Records. *Riverside Low Down* October 11, 1935.
[52] "Company 626" CCC Pictorial Review. *Riverside Low Down* March 13, 1936. "Pick Wardens To Fight Fires" *Journal* March 30, 1939. "Phone Line Will Connect Fire Towers" *Journal* June 29, 1939. Burnett County Forestry Tour, 1937.
[53] "Company 626" *CCC Pictorial Review*. Inspection report February 23, 1934, CCC Program Reports.
[54] *Riverside Low Down* August 30, 1935.
[55] E. C. W. 53-S WORK PROJECTS #60. "Fire Burns 40 Acres In Town of Meenon" *Journal* March 31, 1938. "News From Riverside CCC Camp" *Journal* June 15, 1939.
[56] *Riverside Low Down* July 12, 1935. "Company 626" *CCC Pictorial Review*. E. C. W. 53-S WORK PROJECTS.
[57] Record of Structural Improvements No. 155, January 23, 1939, Conservation Commission Records.
[58] "Company 626" *CCC Sparta District* p40-41. Record of Structural Improvements No. 154, January 23, 1939, Conservation Commission Records. Burnett County Forestry Tour, 1937.
[59] *Riverside Low Down* July 26, 1935.
[60] "Company 626" *CCC Sparta District* p41.
[61] *Riverside Low Down* April 27, 1935. *Riverside Low Down* March, May, June 12, 1936.
[62] "Construction of Ranger Station Started Monday" *Journal* December 1935. *Riverside Low Down* June 12, 1936.
[63] "Will Continue To Operate Civilian Riverside Camp" *Journal* October 7, 1937. "Company 626" *Pictorial Review*. "Co. Board To Consider Establishing Park System" *Journal* October 14, 1937. Work Plan 1937-1938, Conservation Commission Records. Burmeister Interview with Maurice Heyer. *Riverside Low Down* April 10, 1936.
[64] "County Has 76,338 Acres Land Under Forest Crop" *Journal* December 7, 1939. "Company 626" *Pictorial Review*. "128 Residents Make Annual Tour" *Journal* September 23, 1937.
[65] Olson. *Riverside Low Down* September 27, 1935. "Company 626" *CCC Pictorial Review*. "Company 626" *CCC Sparta District* p40. Burnett County Forest History.
[66] *Riverside Low Down* September 25, 1936. Burnett County Forestry Tour 1937. *Riverside Low Down* September 11, 1936. Olson. "Temperature Sizzles At 95 Here Monday For Highest Recording" *Journal* July 25, 1940. Inspection Reports June & October 1935, CCC Program Reports.
[67] *Riverside Low Down* May 10, 1936. Cone Collection Program August 30, 1937, August 11, 1939, Conservation Commission Records. "Will continue To Operate Civilian Riverside Camp" *Journal* October 7, 1937.
[68] *Riverside Low Down* February 1936. "Will Continue To Operate Civilian Riverside Camp" *Journal* October 7, 1937.
[69] *Riverside Low Down*. October 15, 1936. Salmond p122.
[70] *Rivers: Ribbons of Life*.

Endnotes

[71] *Riverside Low Down* February 29, and November 20, 1936. "Company 626" *CCC Sparta District* p41. "Company 626" *CCC Pictorial Review*.
[72] E.C.W. 53-S Work Projects #71. Burmeister interviews with Roy Jarvis and Maurice Heyer 2000. CCC Riverside Lake Improvement Maps for Devils and Big Yellow Lakes. *Riverside Low Down* September 27, 1935.
[73] *Riverside Low Down* July 10, 1936. "Company 626" CCC Sparta District p41. E.C.W. 53-S Work Projects #66
[74] *Riverside Low Down* Aug 30, September 27, October 25, 1935. Inspection Report October 22, 1935, CCC Program Reports. Fure. Interview with Warren Melin.
[75] *Riverside Low Down* July 24, 1936.
[76] *Riverside Low Down* June 12, 1936.
[77] "Act To Restore Water Levels of Northern Lakes" *Journal* August 23, 1934.
[78] "Act To Restore Water Levels of Northern Lakes" *Journal* August 23, 1934.
[79] "Will Build Dams To Raise County Lake Levels" *Journal* April 11, 1935. "County Has 76, 338 Acres Land Under Forest Crop" *Journal* December 7, 1939. "Proposed Lake Project Would Work 80 Men" *Journal* December 9, 1937. "Discuss Survey To Build Dam Across Yellow River" *Journal* March 16, 1939. "Approve Dam To Raise Lake Water Levels" *Journal* December 30, 1937.
[80] "Company 626" *CCC Pictorial Review*. Fure. Interview with Warren Melin.
[81] *Riverside Low Down* November 6, 1936.
[82] "Proposed Lake Project" *Journal* December 9, 1937. "Approve Dam To Raise Lake Water Levels" *Journal* December 30, 1937.
[83] "County Has 76,338 Acres Land Under Forest Crop" *Journal* December 7, 1939.
[84] Neil LeMay Correspondence October 7, November 7, 1939 Conservation Commission Records. CCC Riverside Lake Improvement Maps for Devils and Big Yellow Lakes.
[85] *Riverside Low Down* March 13, 1936.
[86] *Riverside Low Down* October 16, November 6, 1936.
[87] *Riverside Low Down* March 13, April 10, 1936.
[88] "123 Deer County By CCC Boys in County" *Burnett County Enterprise* February 17, 1938.
[89] "Company 626" *CCC Pictorial Review*. "Eight Hundred Pheasants Will be Raised Here" *Journal* June 17, 1937. "1200 Pheasants Released In Various Parts of County" *Journal* September 9, 1937. "Annual Meeting County Sportmen" *Journal* March 17, 1938. "Conservation Club Plans to Increase Pheasant Program" *Journal* March 24, 1938. "Riverside CCC News" *Journal* June 29, 1939.
[90] "County Hopper Invasion Believed Under Control" *Journal* July 2, 1936.
[91] "Riverside CCC News" *Journal* June 29, 1939.
[92] "Hoppers Invade Eastern Towns" *Journal* July 29, 1937.
[93] "Fight The Grasshopper Now" *Journal* June 30, 1938.
[94] "Body of Young Chicagoan Floats To Surface of Lake" *Journal* July 26, 1934. "Body of Hertel Man Found Near Spooner" *Journal* November 19, 1936. "Yellow Lake Man Commits Suicide" *Journal* July 25, 1940. "Drowns When Boat Capsizes in Tabor Lake" *Journal* July 18, 1940.
[95] "History, Sparta District" *CCC Sparta District* p24. "Homeless Flood Victims In Need Of Food, Shelter" *Journal* January 28, 1937. "Flood Victims" *Journal* February 4, 1937. "Danbury Resident Drives Army Truck In Flood Area" *Journal* February 11, 1937. Fure Interview with Helen Quigley.
[96] Index to CCC Regulations Sixth Corps Area, Conservation Commission Records. *Riverside Low Down* July 26, 1935.
[97] *Riverside Low Down* July 26, August 16, 1935, April 24, May 10, June 12, January 30, 1936. Burmeister interview with Maurice Heyer.
[98] Memorandum to Mr. Tinker, Inspection of Wis. ECW Camps April 10, 1934, CCC Program Reports.
[99] Salmon. *Riverside Low Down August* 16, 1935.
[100] *Riverside Low Down* August 14, 1936.
[101] *Riverside Low Down* May 10, 22, June 27, October 16, 1936. Memorandum to Mr. Tinker, Inspection of Wis. ECW Camps April 10, 1934, CCC Program Reports.
[102] *Riverside Low Down* September 13, 1935, May 22, June 12, 1936.
[103] "History, Sparta District" *CCC Sparta District* p189. CCC Riverside Camp Map.
[104] *Riverside Low Down* November 22, 1935, August 14, October 15, 1936.
[105] *Riverside Low Down* August 14, 28, December 18, 1936.
[106] *Riverside Low Down* October 25, 1935, June 27, August 14, October 16, 28 1936. "News From Riverside CCC" *Journal* June 15, 1939.
[107] *Riverside Low Down* February 29, 1936, August 14, 1936, December 18, 1936.
[108] *Riverside Low Down* August 30, 1935, February 29, April 24, May10, 1936.
[109] *Riverside Low Down* July 12, 1935, May 10, June 12, Sept 11, 1936. "Barracks Completed At Ranger Station; Visitors Welcome" *Journal* June 11, 1936.
[110] Fure interview with Harvard Stengal 2000. *Riverside Low Down* October 25, November 8, 1935.
[111] *Riverside Low Down*. Fure. Interview with Warren

Melin.

[112] Memorandum For the Regional Forester July 1, 1934, CCC Program Reports. Inspection Report November 15, 1934, March 9, 1935, CCC Program Reports. "43 Junior CCC Members To Be Enrolled Soon" *Journal* April 25, 1935. "7 Cooks To Be Called To CCC Camps From County" *Journal* May 30, 1935.

[113] Salmond. Cohen p25. "Riverside" *Journal* January 30, 1936. "Danbury" *Journal* March 12, 1936.

[114] Inspection Report October 15, 1936, Conservation Commission Records. Riverside Camp Thanksgiving Menu.

[115] *American Forests*. Salmon p129. Cohen, p54. "Forest Corps To Enlist 100,000 More In October." *Journal* September 13, 1933. Semo p6-8.

[116] "History Sparta District" *CCC Sparta District* p26.

[117] "Danbury" *Journal* May 21, 1936.

[118] "Hospital Notes" *Journal* May 14, 1936. "Grantsburg Hospital News" *Journal* August 27, 1936.

[119] Death Certificate 6-2248.

[120] "Funeral Services Held For Riverside CCC Boy" *Journal* August 31, 1939. Death Certificate 6-2588.

[121] *Riverside Low Down* June 7, July 26, 1935, July 24, 1936. Death Certificates 5-2090, 5-2091.

[122] Salmond, p162. Cohen, p116. "Twenty Nine County boys Enroll At Danbury Camp" *Journal* October 19, 1939.

[123] Cohen, p31. *Riverside Low Down* June 12, 1936. *CCC Pictorial Review*. *American Forests*. *Riverside Low Down* January 30, February 17, March 26, June 12, September 25, 1936.

[124] Inspection Report February 23, 1934, CCC Program Reports.

[125] *Riverside Low Down* July 10, 1936.

[126] Burnett County Schools.

[127] Inspection Report February 23, November 15, 1934, April 16, 1940, CCC Program Reports. *Riverside Low Down* January 30, November 6, December 16, 1936.

[128] *Riverside Low Down* May 22, August 28, 1936.

[129] *Riverside Low Down* May 10, October 16, 1936.

[130] *Riverside Low Down* January 25, September 13, 1935, November 6, 1936.

[131] *Riverside Low Down* July 24, Nov 6, 20, 1936. Semo p9.

[132] *Riverside Low Down* November 6, 20, 1936.

[133] *Riverside Low Down* June 21, 1935.

[134] *Riverside Low Down* September 13, 1935, July 10, September 25, November 6, 1936.

[135] *Riverside Low Down* October 25, 1935.

[136] *Riverside Low Down* June 12, 20, 27, July 10, 1936. "CCC Winners Are Announced." *Superior Evening Telegram* June 22, 1936.

[137] "CCC" http://www.cccalumni.org/states/wisconsin1.html. Salmon. Glad p495-496. Fure Interview with Mrs. Quigley, 2003.

[138] Salmon p143-44.

[139] *Riverside Low Down* November 22, 1935.

[140] Evert Family Papers, letter May 27, 1935.

[141] *Riverside Low Down* September 25, December 18, 1936.

[142] "Danbury" *Journal* November 2, 9, 1933.

[143] *Riverside Low Down* December 18, 1936.

[144] "Riverside Camp Features Entertainment Program." *Journal*, January 18, February 1, 1934. Inspection Report, February 23, 1934, CCC Program Reports.

[145] Fure. Interview with Ivol Paulus, Bert Lund, Russell Stewart, Roy Nordquist, Norris Hoag.

[146] Fure. Interviews with Ivol Paulus, Norris Hoag, Beatrice Olson, Bert Lund, Byron Baker

[147] *Riverside Low Down*.

[148] Inspection Report, February 23, 1934, CCC Program Reports.

[149] Inspection Report, February 23, 1934, CCC Program Reports. *Riverside Low Down* September 13, 27, 1935, January 30, 1936.

[150] "Over $18,000 Paid In County Past Fiscal Year By CCC Camps" *Journal* November 17, 1938.

[151] Riverside Low Down Advertisements. "History Sparta District CCC." *CCC Sparta District*.

[152] *Riverside Low Down* Advertisements.

[153] Olson. "Ten New Indian Homes Dedicated At Danbury." *Journal* September 22, 1938. "Build Modern Indian Homes At Sand Lake." *Journal* February 9, 1939. Burnett County Forest History. Wisconsin Conservation Department Timber Sale Report, Sale No.1. Official Proceedings of the Burnett County Board of Commissioners 1937.

[154] "Forestry Tour Meets With Signal Success" *Burnett County Enterprise* August 20, 1936. "128 Residents Make Annual Tour of Burnett County Forest Lands" *Journal* September 23, 1937. "Forestry Tour Through Burnett, Other Counties" *Journal* July 6, 1939. "Invite Public to Visit Camp Riverside" *Journal* March 28, 1940. Inspection Report August 21, 1936, Conservation Commission Records. *Riverside Low Down* July 10, 1936. "Crowd of 3000 Celebrate At Danbury July 4th" *Journal* July 9, 1936. Burnett County Forest History.

[155] "First County School Forest Will Be Planted Today" *Journal* September 23, 1937. *Riverside Low Down* September 25, 1936.

[156] "Twenty-one Tree Planting Demonstrations Last Week" *Journal* April 25, 1940.

[157] "Plant Fourteen Million Fish In County Lakes" *Journal* March 9, 1939. "27 Million Fish Planted In Co. Lakes, Streams" *Journal* June 27, 1940.

[158] "Burnett Leads Wisconsin In Tree Planting"

Journal April 18, 1940. "Burnett Leads State In Reforestation Light Soil" *Journal* June 20, 1940.

[159] Salmond p129, 132. Glad p494-5, 498-9.

[160] Lewis. "CCC: $1-a-day, Work Welcomed" Unidentified Newspaper clipping.

[161] Pearson. "Foresters hold open house." *Inter-County Leader*, Burnett Section. August 11, 1993.

[162] *Riverside Low Down* September 25, 1936.

[163] Fure Interview with Mrs. Helen Quigley 2003. Quigley, Francis John, Personnel Record. "John F. Quigley" Obituary *Burnett County Sentinel* December 12, 2001. Land Record Burnett County Register of Deeds. "Wisconsin Conservation Corps, CCC Alumni attend." *Inter-County Leader* February 29, 1984. Lewis. "CCC: $1-a-day, Work Welcome" Unidentified Newspaper clipping. "Foresters hold open house at Camp Burnett." *Leader*, Burnett County Section August 11, 1993.

[164] "Burnett Applies For Additional CCC Camps" *Journal* April 4, 1935.

[165] *Riverside Low Down* February 29, 1936. *Superior Evening Telegram* article reprinted in *Riverside Low Down* October 16, 1936. Salmond p184. Sixteenth Biennial Report of the Wis. C. C. 1937-1938, Conservation Commission Records. "Four Years Old, the CCC Now Looks Ahead to a Permanent Setup" *Journal* June 3, 1937.

[166] Fure. Interview with Norris Hoag. "C.C.C. Camp At St. Croix Falls Ordered Closed." *Siren Leader* December 2, 1937.

[167] "Will Disband Riverside CCC Last of Month" *Journal* September 16, 1937 "May Continue Riverside CCC" *Journal* September 23, 1937. "Will Continue To Operate Civilian Riverside Camp" *Journal* October 7, 1937. "Danbury" *Journal* July 18, 1935.

[168] Cohen p153.

[169] Salmond p184. Motion to Keep Riverside Camp Open, September 15, 1937, Conservation Commission Records. Priority List of CCC Camps December 13, 1937, Conservation Commission Records. Wisconsin Conservation Bulletin December-January 1937-1938, Conservation Commission Records.

[170] Salmond p184. "Vacancies Still Exist In the U.S. Army" *Journal* January 13, 1938. "U.S. Army Again Seeks Applicants For Service" *Journal* June 2, 1938. "County Quota Set At 30 For Forest Project" *Journal* May 4, 1933. "Will Give Vets Preference In CCC Enrollment" *Journal* April 19, 1934. "CCC Camps Offer Free Training For Industry" *Journal* June 19, 1941. "Enroll 15 In Riverside CCC Camp At Danbury" *Journal* January 18, 1940.

[171] Salmond p184. Cohen p24. Information Pertaining to Enrollment April 14, 1937, Conservation Commission Records. "Extend CCC Age Limit" *Journal* May 9, 1935. "County CCC Replacement From June 15 to August 31" *Journal* May 30, 1935. "7th CCC Enrollment At Public Welfare Office" *Journal* March 26, 1936. "25 Enrolled In Riverside CCC" *Journal* April 13, 1939. "Take Application For Enrollment In CCC Camp" *Journal* June 20, 1940. "CCC Camps Will Take Enrollment Any Time" *Journal* August 21, 1941.

[172] Salmond p184.

[173] Inspection Report June 10, 1937, Conservation Commission Records.

[174] Evert Family Papers, letter July 5, 1938.

[175] Danbury Fire Investigation Report.

[176] Fure. Interviews with Norris Hoag and Ivol Paulus, Byron Baker.

[177] "News From Riverside CCC Camp" *Journal* June 15, 1939. Cohen p128-29. Salmond p196-7.

[178] Salmond p211, 215-16. Cohen p128-29.

[179] Semo p14.

[180] Fure Interview with Maurice Heyer, 2003.

About the Author

Retired from nursing, Carole moved with her husband John to their summer home in Burnett County. Retirement offered Carole free time to pursue her interests in history, quilting, and writing, three hobbies which often merge.

Carole enjoys the stories found in historical research and has written several family histories. Her writing expanded to include quilting which resulted in her first publication, *Creative Designs from Traditional Quilt Blocks*.

As a volunteer in the Burnett County Historical Society's history research library, Carole had the opportunity to investigate the story of the Riverside CCC Camp near Danbury. "Once I started I couldn't stop until the story was told," she said *The Power of Sand, Burnett County and the Civilian Conservation Corps* is the result of that research.

Carole continues to pursue ideas relevant to her melded hobbies and looks forward to her next project.